DEVOTIONS & PRAYERS
for Managing
ANXIETY & DEPRESSION

TRISHA WHITE PRIEBE

DEVOTIONS & PRAYERS for Managing ANXIETY + DEPRESSION

COMFORT &
ENCOURAGEMENT
FOR TEEN GIRLS

BARBOUR
PUBLISHING

© 2024 by Barbour Publishing, Inc.

Print ISBN 978-1-63609-828-9

All rights reserved. No part of this publication may be reproduced or transmitted for commercial purposes, except for brief quotations in printed reviews, without written permission of the publisher. Reproduced text may not be used on the World Wide Web. No Barbour Publishing content may be used as artificial intelligence training data for machine learning, or in any similar software development.

Churches and other noncommercial interests may reproduce portions of this book without the express written permission of Barbour Publishing, provided that the text does not exceed 500 words or 5 percent of the entire book, whichever is less, and that the text is not material quoted from another publisher. When reproducing text from this book, include the following credit line: "From *Devotions and Prayers for Managing Anxiety and Depression: Comfort and Encouragement for Teen Girls*, published by Barbour Publishing, Inc. Used by permission."

Unless otherwise indicated, all scripture quotations are taken from the New Life Version copyright © 1969 and 2003 by Barbour Publishing, Inc., Uhrichsville, Ohio, 44683. All rights reserved.

Scripture quotations marked niv are taken from the Holy Bible, New International Version®. niv®. Copyright © 1973, 1978, 1984, 2011 by Biblica, Inc.™ Used by permission. All rights reserved worldwide.

Scripture quotations marked esv are from The Holy Bible, English Standard Version®, copyright © 2001 by Crossway Bibles, a publishing ministry of Good News Publishers. The esv® text has been reproduced in cooperation with and by permission of Good News Publishers. Unauthorized reproduction of this publication is prohibited. All rights reserved.

Cover Design: Greg Jackson, Thinkpen Design

Published by Barbour Publishing, Inc., 1810 Barbour Drive, Uhrichsville, Ohio 44683, www.barbourbooks.com

Our mission is to inspire the world with the life-changing message of the Bible.

Printed in the United States of America.

To Jillian

If the research is right that daughters are seven times more likely to deal with anxiety if their mothers struggle with it, this is my honest attempt to help you tell a better story.

LET'S START HERE

"I have told you these things so you may have peace in Me. In the world you will have much trouble. But take hope! I have power over the world!"
JOHN 16:33

Anxiety and depression are big topics, and we have lots to discuss in these pages, but let's start here. I want you to know three important things from the beginning: *Life is hard. You are hurting. I believe you.*

It's hard being a teenage girl in today's world. In just a few pages, we'll discuss a few of the reasons why. In the meantime, I want you to know you aren't alone in your struggle, and you're right where you belong. By picking up a book like this, you're showing incredible courage.

In John 16, Jesus told His followers that life would be very hard for them. Jesus wanted His followers to know that just because their lives were difficult, that didn't necessarily mean they were doing something wrong. He also wanted them to understand that He had power over everything troubling them.

As we begin this study, be encouraged that the same truth applies to *you*.

Father, as I begin this new journey, I ask for Your guidance and blessing. Please give me courage and clarity to learn and apply what You show me. Amen.

FEAR FACTOR

Give all your worries to Him because He cares for you.
1 PETER 5:7

Before we define *anxiety* and *depression*, we need to talk about *fear* and *worry*.

Did you know *fear* is considered one of the five basic emotions of survival? Healthy expressions of fear cause us to look both ways before crossing the street and to answer the door cautiously when a stranger knocks. Unhealthy—or sinful—expressions of fear cause us to doubt the promises of God or make choices that are inconsistent with His Word.

Worry is when we spend time lingering on the things we fear. It's the difference between visiting a city on vacation or choosing to stay and rent a home there. Instead of allowing fears to come and go as fleeting thoughts that we answer with God's truth, we linger on them. *What if something bad happens to my family? What if nobody likes me?*

To hope for the day when we're not afraid of anything is to hope for a day that will never come until heaven. But letting those fears run the show is another matter.

Whenever we're afraid, we have an invitation to look to God.

Father, You have invited me to give You all my worries. Please remind me to seek You whenever I am afraid. Thank You for caring about me. Amen.

THE WAR AGAINST WORRY

*"Which of you can make himself a
little taller by worrying?"*
MATTHEW 6:27

So much of anxiety and depression is actually a war against worry.

Assuming our brains are otherwise healthy—which we'll talk about soon—if we could stop worry in its tracks, we would more easily win our battles with anxiety and depression.

Worry adds absolutely nothing of value. One of the reasons we worry is because it *feels* like we are doing something to prevent what we're worried about. But in reality, we're not accomplishing anything helpful. This is why—in Jesus' famous Sermon on the Mount—He asks His audience, "Which one of you can make yourself taller by worrying about your height?" (my paraphrase). The obvious answer then and now is *nobody*.

Worry doesn't actually fix anything.

Here's what worry creates: inadequate sleep, persistent headaches, growing irritability, and poor concentration. And there's *still* no guarantee that the thing we're worried about will be avoided.

God never says, "Don't worry; nothing bad will happen to you." But He does say we can trust Him no matter what happens, for He is trustworthy.

> Father, You never instruct me to live a careless life, but You do invite me to live a carefree life as I trust and understand that You have my best interests in mind. Amen.

ANXIETY DEFINED

"Do not worry about tomorrow. Tomorrow will have its own worries. The troubles we have in a day are enough for one day."
MATTHEW 6:34

So if *worry* is what happens when we linger on the things we fear, *anxiety* is what happens when our fears or worries get stuck in our brains. Sometimes this fear actually starts to feel like it's looping in our brains—like the words on a digital sign in front of a bank or church building.

In an earlier devotion, we distinguished *worry* from *fear* as being the difference between visiting a city on vacation and choosing to rent a home there. But anxiety takes fear even further. If worry rents a home, anxiety actually buys the house and moves in permanently.

Anxiety is fear that gets stuck in your heart and mind.

Often when we're experiencing anxiety, we're seeing the problem as bigger than it actually is; and if we're seeing a solution at all, we're seeing it as much smaller than it actually is.

Here's the spoiler: God is bigger than any of your anxieties or fears. And if you ask Him to help you, *He will*.

Father, when fears begin to loop in my brain, please help me identify what's happening and turn to You for help. I have a lot to be anxious about if I refuse to surrender those anxieties to You. Amen.

THIS IS DEPRESSION

*Even the darkness is not dark to You.
And the night is as bright as the day.
Darkness and light are the same to You.*
PSALM 139:12

In the last devotion, we defined anxiety. So, what is *depression*?

The longer we live, the more fears we accumulate. We learn new ways we could be hurt, for example, or we face the agonizing reality that those we love could be harmed.

If we regularly revisit those fears—however real or imaginary—they morph into *worry*. If the worries get stuck in our minds, they become *anxiety*. And if the anxiety goes unhandled, it can become *depression*.

Have you ever worn sunglasses inside a house? Everything suddenly becomes dark, and it's hard to see things the way they actually look. *Depression* can start to feel like wearing sunglasses inside. Nothing is bright or hopeful—everything is covered in dark shadows.

The enemy loves when we get to this point because it becomes hard for us to see God and His good gifts as they are intended to be in our lives.

But here's what I know to be true: it takes hard work to undo anxiety and depression, but it is absolutely possible. The first step is believing that God *can* and *will* deliver us if we ask Him.

> Father, please help me clearly see You and Your goodness in my life today. Amen.

DIGGING UP THE ROOTS

"Do not fear, for I am with you. Do not be afraid, for I am your God. I will give you strength, and for sure I will help you. Yes, I will hold you up with My right hand that is right and good."
ISAIAH 41:10

Being able to identify where your anxiety is coming from can be the first step toward finding freedom from it. We can't discuss solutions until we uncover the roots.

So where do anxiety and depression come from? Short answer: they can come from *internal* or *external* challenges.

By now you probably understand that there are many contributing factors to your anxiety or depression. It is complicated and complex. Your life—with all its beautiful characters and strange plot twists—is uniquely yours. Nobody else in the world has your specific story.

Your reasons for battling anxiety or depression could be physical, relational, or moral. We'll look at each of these briefly in the next few devotions and see how they apply to your situation.

But for now, understand this: God has promised to help you with whatever you're feeling and facing. You never need to handle your anxiety or depression alone. I'm going to ask you to take a risk with me and trust that God is big enough to fix what's broken. *You in?*

Father, thank You that I do not need to handle my fears by myself. Amen.

THE ANXIOUS BRAIN

Do you not know that your body is a house of God where the Holy Spirit lives? God gave you His Holy Spirit. Now you belong to God. You do not belong to yourselves.
1 CORINTHIANS 6:19

Your battle with anxiety or depression could be *physical*.

Please hear me carefully: your battle could be biological and require medical treatment from a doctor. Sometimes the neurons and synapses in our brains don't fire properly and can lead to chemical imbalances.

Also, some medical conditions—including thyroid problems and various vitamin deficiencies—can mimic depression symptoms. So it's important to talk to a doctor to help rule out physical issues that could be easily treated.

Since I'm not a doctor, I'm not going to address this in further detail, other than to encourage you to be a good steward of your body and health. If you need to talk to a doctor, don't hesitate to do so. Your body—including your brain—is especially important because the Holy Spirit dwells in the body of every child of God.

But here's some much-needed good news for you and for me: ongoing research continues to confirm that the brain is adaptable all through life.

> As the Great Physician, You see what is causing my anxious brain. Please give me the wisdom to ask for help when I need it. Amen.

THE FRIEND ZONE

Nothing should be done because of pride or thinking about yourself. Think of other people as more important than yourself.
PHILIPPIANS 2:3

Your battle with anxiety and depression could be *relational*.

As human beings, we were made to connect with other people. The Bible tells us we were made in the image of our triune God (Genesis 1:26), and the Trinity is an eternal fellowship of the Father, Son, and Holy Spirit.

So your desire to be loved and accepted? That's not a bad thing. As you'll see in the coming pages, we're *made* for connection and belonging. Therefore, it's wise and natural to want good relationships with people.

But sometimes social pressure or the desire to fit in creates anxiety. When people in our lives are unkind or cruel, for example, that can be hard to understand. Our past experiences—good or bad—can have a big impact on how we move forward in building friendships or approaching relationships.

Later in this book, we'll learn how to respond to relational hurts in our lives.

Bottom line: relationships in this lifetime can be such reliable heartbreakers. But there *are* good friends out there, and with time you *can* find them.

Father, please help me choose friends wisely, and please help me be a true friend to those You put in my path. Amen.

SOUL DEEP

*"He who listens to me will live free from danger,
and he will rest easy from the fear of what is sinful."*
PROVERBS 1:33

Your battle with anxiety and depression could be *moral*.

I am not saying that you are living in sin and so your anxiety and depression are a result of sin. I don't have the right to make that claim.

I am saying that we live in a world that is absolutely wrecked by sin. So your anxiety or depression could be the result of sin done *to* you, sin done *by* you, or sin done *around* you.

As we've seen in previous devotions, anxiety and depression are often more than a spiritual issue, but they are never less than a spiritual issue, because everything affects our spiritual life.

Because of that, the rest of this book is going to focus primarily on your spiritual life—not because I don't think there are other components, but because I believe your spiritual life is critically important in this fight. I want to be a voice of encouragement to you.

Fighting anxiety and depression is a spiritual battle, but thankfully—as we'll see in the coming pages—God has given you the right tools for this battle.

> Father, if there's something in my life that needs to change, please draw my attention to it. Amen.

HIDE-AND-SEEK

Look through me, O God, and know my heart. Try me and know my thoughts. See if there is any sinful way in me and lead me in the way that lasts forever.
PSALM 139:23–24

We cannot heal what we hide. Put another way, we cannot move through what we refuse to acknowledge.

Thankfully, there is no safer place or person than God, and He invites you to be absolutely honest with Him about what you're feeling and facing. *He already knows because He knows everything, so you won't surprise Him.* Tell Him about your loneliness. Talk to Him about the peer pressure. Ask Him to help you with your schoolwork.

God is omniscient, meaning He knows everything there is to know about you. From the deepest thoughts and desires of your heart to the tiniest details of your life, He knows it all. *And He loves you.*

If you're ready to get really honest about the anxiety or depression in your life, a good place to start is coming to God with open hands and a humble heart and asking Him for help and healing.

Nothing is wasted when you take your concerns to God. And in return, you are the most secure you will ever be when you believe God's words are true.

> Father, I believe You. I trust You. I love You. Amen.

SHATTERING

"I have told you these things so you may have peace in Me. In the world you will have much trouble. But take hope! I have power over the world!"
John 16:33

Trauma is a Greek word that means "injury." In its simplest definition, *trauma* is a deeply internal response to a painful or tragic event. It can feel like a shattering.

Studies say that by the time we turn sixteen years old, most of us will have experienced a traumatic event. This event can include anything from the loss of someone we love to a shocking situation that we witness. It can be something that happens to us that should not happen. It can also be something that doesn't happen to us but should have happened.

Each of us responds to traumatic events differently. After being cracked open by a life-changing moment, some of us are able to acknowledge the pain and carry on with our lives. Others take longer to move forward. And sometimes we respond to trauma by *trying harder*. We may think if we work harder, we'll avoid being hurt in the future.

Know this: God is committed to healing every bit of trauma you've experienced. Nothing is outside the reach of His redemption.

> Father, You have been my rock and my refuge during the hardest moments of my life. Thank You.

LIAR, LIAR

I pray that you will know how great His power is for those who have put their trust in Him.
EPHESIANS 1:19

When we're afraid, we're exactly where our enemy wants us. He loves nothing more than to catch us in a moment of anxiety, devastation, or depression. It's in those moments that he can more easily lie to us. *And we'll more easily believe what he says.*

Here are two things anxiety and depression are afraid of: *being powerless* and *being alone*. But ironically, anxiety and depression *leave us* feeling powerless and alone. The enemy, however, isn't going to tell you that.

He's not going to tell you that anxiety can lead to a constant state of hypervigilance, making it hard to make good decisions. He's also not going to tell you that anxiety can lead you to withdraw from healthy social interactions, creating a sense of isolation. He would rather have you believe that anxiety is out of your control and will never get any better.

But the enemy is a liar.

If you are a child of God, God's power exists for you to draw upon, and His presence in your life is a guarantee—which means you are never powerless or alone.

> Father, I know the enemy's primary strategy is lies. Please help me identify when I'm believing the enemy instead of You. Amen.

PLAYING IT SAFE

*The pains given by a friend are faithful,
but the kisses of one who hates you are false.*
PROVERBS 27:6

Not everything comforting is helpful, and not everything helpful is comforting.

As human beings, we're wired to seek comfort at all cost. We naturally gravitate toward familiar, safe routines and relationships. We work hard to maintain a sense of security, both physically and emotionally.

But no matter how good it feels, comfort isn't always our friend. The world is full of counterfeit comforts, including self-destructive behaviors and toxic relationships.

Personal and spiritual growth most often happens outside our comfort zone.

An important part of responding biblically to anxiety and depression is learning to get comfortable being uncomfortable. This plan may include pursuing difficult conversations or being honest with ourselves or others. Making good changes can feel really uncomfortable at first.

But it's helpful to keep in mind that anxiety is already making us uncomfortable. So the type of discomfort we're seeking isn't bad—it'll actually prove to be very good in the end, especially if we can retrain our brains and bodies. The key is acknowledging the discomfort and pressing forward anyway.

> Father, belonging to You is my greatest source of comfort. Help me to remember this truth as I try to do necessary, hard things. Amen.

THE GOSPEL TRUTH

He was hurt for our wrong-doing. He was crushed for our sins. He was punished so we would have peace. He was beaten so we would be healed.
ISAIAH 53:5

The answer to our anxiety isn't trying harder. Trying harder doesn't result in courage—trust does. But what or whom we trust makes all the difference.

No matter what you're facing, the gospel is powerful enough to address and embrace any hardship you have. If you're a follower of Christ, the gospel doesn't just save you for eternity—it also keeps you and sustains you every day of your life.

So, what is the gospel? It's the good news that Jesus died for our sin, rose again, and triumphed over death and evil so that there is no condemnation for those who trust in Him.

The gospel offers us a far better story than self-sufficiency. At the heart of what it means to be a follower of Christ is receiving a new identity. And this new identity changes everything.

Your past choices, habits, traumas, or relationships may try to condemn you, but as a child of God, *you are not condemned*. You are seen, known, and safe. So, let's look at each of these briefly in the next three devotions.

> Father, help me understand that the gospel is big enough to embrace every issue in my life. Amen.

A NOTE ON BEING SEEN

*See, the eye of the Lord is on those who fear Him,
and on those who hope for His loving-kindness.*
PSALM 33:18

What does it mean to be *seen*?

Recently, I needed to go to the mailbox late at night. But I live in the country where it gets really dark, and I can often hear animals howling in the distance. At first, I stepped out of my house a little afraid, but then I noticed my husband, Luke, standing at the front door watching as I went. And suddenly my fear disappeared.

To *be seen* is more than simply *being observed*. It includes being recognized, acknowledged, and understood by someone who cares.

Genesis 16 tells the story of a woman named Hagar who experienced deep pain as a result of the bad decisions made for her by others. Hagar believed she and her child would die alone. But God came to talk to her and promise His protection, and in their conversation, Hagar was so moved by God's kindness that she famously said, "You are the God who sees me" (Genesis 16:13 NIV).

The same God who saw Hagar sees you. The way I could walk in the dark without fear is the way you can walk confidently through life—because God sees you.

> Father, thank You for seeing me.
> Please help me learn to see others with
> compassion and kindness. Amen.

THE ART OF BEING KNOWN

*The Lord is good, a safe place in times of trouble.
And He knows those who come to Him to be safe.*
NAHUM 1:7

What does it mean to be *known*?

What could you talk about for twenty minutes without doing any research? What's a topic you know well? Music? Books? Baking? Math?

Did you know God could talk about *you* endlessly? He made you, loves you, and knows you better than you know yourself.

"Are not two small birds sold for a very small piece of money? And yet not one of the birds falls to the earth without your Father knowing it. God knows how many hairs you have on your head. So do not be afraid. You are more important than many small birds" (Matthew 10:29–31).

Maybe you're wondering, *But how on earth does it help my anxiety to know God knows me?*

Good question. Answer: if God made us and knows us even better than we know ourselves, we should pay attention to what He says will help us in this world. Talk to Him. If you knew His heart for you, you would.

Father, I am humbled and comforted knowing that I am fully known by You. In You I find true acceptance and belonging. Amen.

SAFETY FIRST

*The Lord will keep you from all that is sinful.
He will watch over your soul. The Lord will watch
over your coming and going, now and forever.*
PSALM 121:7–8

What does it mean to be *safe*?

Most people would probably answer the question by saying something like, "I want to have my basic needs met and my biggest risks minimized."

But is that really what makes us feel safe?

Often, when we're anxious, what we think we want to know is what will happen in the future. But what we actually want to know is what will still be true no matter what happens in the future. Put another way, our future isn't usually what scares us as much as who will love us no matter what.

Here's what will always be true in your life: God will still be good, and He will still love you.

The first question of the 1563 Heidelberg Catechism asks, "What is your only comfort in life and death?" And then the answer is "That I am not my own, but belong with body and soul, both in life and in death, to my faithful Savior Jesus Christ...."

Because of that, you are safe.

> Father, thank You for keeping me safe. When I am afraid, remind me that You are with me. Amen.

MULTIPLE CHOICE

*There are many plans in a man's heart,
but it is the Lord's plan that will stand.*
PROVERBS 19:21

Wouldn't it be nice if life were simply a series of choices—that if we did and said the right things, then the right outcomes would always occur?

If I'm nice, I'll have lots of friends.
If I invite people to my house, I'll be invited to theirs.
If I do my best, I will get good grades.

But as you know by now, life is a lot more complicated than that, and there are many things we can't control, even if we make the right choices.

Control is a fake relationship. We can't make people like us. We can't control outcomes. The Bible tells us we don't even have the power to make ourselves a little taller (Matthew 6:27).

This definitely doesn't feel like good news, but here's what's infinitely good: God is the one who is writing your story, and He has promised to keep writing until the final chapter is good. If you understood His great love for you, you would not keep trying to take His pen away.

You must learn to trust Him with it.

Father, I know You are the only one truly in control of all things, and every choice You make for me is good. Amen.

DECODING EMOTIONS

Trust in Him at all times, O people. Pour out your heart before Him. God is a safe place for us.
PSALM 62:8

Think of your emotions like text messages:

They often come uninvited.

They usually contain small bits of information—sometimes helpful, sometimes not.

The owner of the phone gets to decide how to respond.

Likewise, your emotions are messengers. They are meant to report back to you what is happening in your heart, but they aren't meant to be your boss.

Emotions aren't bad or good, but how we choose to respond to our emotions can be right or wrong. Underneath every emotion is a message for us to decode.

Angry? Why am I so upset?

Sad? What do I think I need to be happy?

Afraid? Of whom or what am I so fearful?

Emotions aren't an enemy. We were made by God to have and experience emotions. Some Bible scholars believe Jesus displayed more than thirty different emotions in the Gospels. So instead of avoiding emotion, we should come NEAR: *name* the emotion, *examine* it, *ask* questions, and *respond* to it.

Your emotions are safest when they are entrusted to the one who loves you perfectly.

Father, because unexpressed emotions can turn into anxiety, I pray that You would give me courage to bring my emotions to You for help. Amen.

RUNNING SCARED

When I am afraid, I will trust in You.
PSALM 56:3

Speaking of emotions, let's talk about fear.

You feel the rush of adrenaline. Your heart begins to race, and your breathing becomes shallow. Your palms grow sweaty, and your body tenses. Maybe you even feel a knot in the pit of your stomach. *You know fear.*

Fear is a powerful emotion that arises in response to a perceived threat or danger. Fear itself is not a bad or sinful thing. But what we *do* with our fear makes all the difference. The earlier we stop fear in its tracks, the less likely it will be to loop in our brains and become anxiety.

My earliest memories as a child involve fear. I was afraid of everything from going to sleep at night to losing the people I love the most. What has changed as I've gotten older isn't my ability *not to fear anything* but, instead, my ability *to trust God more* than I fear bad things happening. Because I do not want to be a prisoner to my own worst fears and imaginings, I choose to put my trust in God.

> Father, because fear can shut down thinking and amp up feeling, I pray You would help me trust You in moments when I'm afraid.

TRUE OR FALSE

"You will know the truth and the truth will make you free."
JOHN 8:32

In the fight against anxiety and depression, truth is incredibly important. Anxiety often thrives on distorted thoughts and irrational beliefs.

Knowing the truth and *telling* the truth—even and especially to ourselves—is critically important in the battle against anxiety and depression. Life begins to change when we become more committed to truth than we are to comfort.

But identifying truth isn't always as easy as it sounds. Lots of people will tell you lots of things that sound believable.

In this book, you and I are on a truth-finding mission. I don't want you to assume anything I say in these pages is right or wrong. I want you to dig into your Bible and find out for yourself. Psalm 119:160 says, "All of Your Word is truth, and every one of Your laws, which are always right, will last forever."

We must learn to tell the truth about God. *What has He said? What has He promised?* We must learn to tell the truth about ourselves. *Who is in control of my life? What does that mean?*

Let's spend the next two devotions talking about two specific truths you should know for sure.

> Father, thank You that all of Your words are true. Help me live like I believe You. Amen.

SALT IN THE WOUND

We do not look at the things that can be seen.
We look at the things that cannot be seen.
The things that can be seen will come to an end.
But the things that cannot be seen will last forever.
2 CORINTHIANS 4:18

Truth one: *this pain will not last forever*.

This is one of the enemy's favorite tricks. He wants you to believe that whatever hard situation or feeling you're experiencing right now *will* last forever. This simply isn't true.

The pain, though intense, is a passing scene in the story of your life. Often, what can feel big and overwhelming to us doesn't even end up being that significant when we look back on it later. Wounds heal. What truly *is* big and overwhelming won't always feel as intense as it does in the moment.

Pain can create a distorted sense of time. It can also convince us that we're permanently stuck in our current situation, unable to ever move forward or move on. But none of this is true.

Yes, you may feel overwhelmed right now. Maybe you're embarrassed, ashamed, lonely, or sad. Hold on to hope, look for support in safe people, and trust God to fix whatever is broken.

With God, you are never ever hopeless.

> Father, with You I always have hope.
> Help me to remember that when I'm tempted
> to believe things will never get better. Amen.

TOGETHER FOREVER

You have never been tempted to sin in any different way than other people. God is faithful. He will not allow you to be tempted more than you can take. But when you are tempted, He will make a way for you to keep from falling into sin.
1 CORINTHIANS 10:13

Truth two: *you are not alone.*

Specifically, when it comes to anxiety, you aren't alone in facing it or in experiencing it—not even close.

Researchers believe anxiety levels are at an all-time high. The fast-paced nature of our current culture, the unpredictability of our global events, and the unbelievable speed of our technological advancements have contributed to heightened anxiety on a national and international level.

We are often tempted to believe we're alone with whatever we're feeling or facing. And when we believe this lie, we hide when we're struggling—and that's actually when we most need to be with trusted people who will help point us to truth.

Courage is not meant to be cultivated on our own.

Know this: anxiety doesn't get the final word. God says there are solutions to the deepest needs of our hearts and minds, and one of those solutions is community.

> Father, thank You for the people You've placed in my life. Help me see and appreciate them as the gift they are. Amen.

ALONE TIME

*"Have I not told you? Be strong and have strength
of heart! Do not be afraid or lose faith. For the
Lord your God is with you anywhere you go."*
JOSHUA 1:9

Anxiety and depression are isolating. One of our enemy's great strategies for keeping us from getting the help and support we need is to make us believe we are alone in our struggle.

But God is with you. *I know. . . . You probably expected me to say this.* But it's true. And it can't be underestimated. The same God of David, Gideon, the disciples in the boat, Esther, Daniel. . .is with *you* too. You matter to God as much as any person in the Bible.

In Joshua 1, Moses had just died, and God was telling Joshua that he was now in charge of leading the children of Israel. As God talked to Joshua, He said the words with which many Christians have encouraged their own hearts: "Be strong and have strength of heart! Do not be afraid or lose faith. . . . God is with you anywhere you go."

God would not be God if He failed you. He won't do it. He'll keep every promise He has ever made.

> Father, thank You for reminding me that I
> am never alone, even when I feel lonely.

THE TRUTH THAT CHANGES EVERYTHING

O taste and see that the Lord is good.
How happy is the man who trusts in Him!
PSALM 34:8

If all we knew about God is that He is in control, that wouldn't necessarily be enough of a reason to trust Him. History is filled with controlling men who did unspeakably evil things.

But the truth that changes everything is this: not only is God in control, but He is also *good*.

At some point, you must decide for yourself whether you believe God is good. Your conclusion either way has the potential to change everything about the way you view yourself and your anxiety.

If God is good, then everything He tells you in the Bible is for your good and can be trusted. If He is not good, then the Bible can't be trusted and all of us are left to figure everything out for ourselves.

Here's what I believe with all my heart: God is much better than you or I can imagine. He is not a set of beliefs—He's a person. Someone worth getting to know and love. He is completely trustworthy. And my prayer for you is that you will find this to be true.

> Father, the better I get to know You,
> the better I'll learn to trust You.
> So help me know You better. Amen.

BY THE NUMBERS

*"Peace I leave with you. My peace I give to you.
I do not give peace to you as the world gives.
Do not let your hearts be troubled or afraid."*
JOHN 14:27

You aren't alone, because God is with you. But you're also not alone statistically.

Did you know girls are twice as likely as boys to deal with anxiety?

Hormonal changes, academic pressures, social media, peer relationships, body image issues, and cultural expectations can all contribute to heightened levels of anxiety in teenage girls. We'll talk more specifically in the next few devotions about some of these particular areas.

First, though, understand that what you are feeling and facing doesn't make you unusual. *It's normal.* Some statistics suggest that as many as three out of five teenage girls face persistent anxiety. So when you're in a room of girls your age, you are not alone in the fight with anxiety.

I wrote every word in this book because I too want to meet you right here and remind you that hope is always pursuing you. You never need to be alone in your fight against anxiety. You have everything you need to overcome it.

> Father, it's hard being a teen girl,
> but thank You for giving me everything
> I need to overcome anxiety. Amen.

REDEFINING BEAUTY

I will give thanks to You, for the greatness of the way I was made brings fear. Your works are great and my soul knows it very well.
PSALM 139:14

Let's talk about body image and our culture's obsession with impossible beauty standards. Recently, I found a dress at a local thrift shop with a tag on the inside that said "This dress was made by hand with great love."

Likewise, *you* were made by hand with great love by the same God who formed the earth. God carefully and precisely knit you together in your mother's womb. Have you ever considered how it hurts the heart of God to see the way we women—young and old—pick apart our appearances? When we dislike something about ourselves, we're ultimately disliking something God created.

Our world has a warped view of what beauty entails. In addition to using unrealistic ideals of beauty as a measure of worth, we've completely lost sight of what God says is beautiful.

First Peter 3:4 says, "Your beauty should come from the inside. It should come from the heart. This is the kind that lasts. Your beauty should be a gentle and quiet spirit. In God's sight this is of great worth and no amount of money can buy it."

> Father, please help me learn to see myself the way You see me. Amen.

TIME-OUT

I will set no sinful thing in front of my eyes. I hate the work of those who are not faithful. It will not get hold of me.
Psalm 101:3

Let's talk about social media.

Technology is never neutral. Whether we're talking about movies, music, or the internet—what we put into our minds has the power to shape the way we think.

Yes, there is value in virtual connection and shared information, but social media also invites us to constantly measure ourselves against carefully curated online personas. And excessive social media usage can actually hinder real-life relationships and lead to anxiety.

We talked in an earlier devotion about being seen. Social media—despite how it feels at times—doesn't actually *see* or *know* you. Social media sees and knows only the version of you that you present to the world—and the same is true of the people whose lives you look at on social media.

To be seen and known in real life by real people requires that we take a time-out from technology and have face-to-face conversations with people who care. We must mindfully set personal boundaries and pursue genuine connections away from technology that are far more beneficial.

It may not be easy, but it's healthy.

> Father, help me learn to say no and step away when it would be helpful. Amen.

JOMO

Even more than that, I think of everything as worth nothing. It is so much better to know Christ Jesus my Lord. I have lost everything for Him. And I think of these things as worth nothing so that I can have Christ.
PHILIPPIANS 3:8

You've probably heard the term FOMO—the fear of missing out. I want to introduce you to JOMO—the *joy* of missing out.

We can actually learn to replace FOMO-induced anxiety with JOMO—a delightful break from constant social pressures. By choosing to say no to some invitations or opportunities, we can pursue other invitations or opportunities to cultivate deeper connection and focus on activities that bring genuine joy and fulfillment.

Yes, there are actually benefits to missing out on some things. In an era of constant social engagement and digital overload, we can choose to pause, recharge, and prioritize the choices that result in our greatest good and God's greatest glory. JOMO gives you the pleasure of saying no to commitment overload and creating space for personal growth and meaningful connection.

By embracing JOMO, we learn to discover the profound joy that comes from choosing how we'll spend our time instead of allowing our time to decide how it will spend us.

> Father, please give me wisdom to know what opportunities I should pursue and which invitations I should graciously decline. Amen.

THE THIEF OF JOY

Everyone should live the life the Lord gave to him.
1 CORINTHIANS 7:17

Let's talk about comparison.

Your unique life is a gift from God. Not only does comparison distract us from the assignment God has given us but it's a slippery slope that leads to discontentment. Constantly measuring ourselves against other girls' achievements, appearance, or lifestyles creates an unhealthy cycle of dissatisfaction that robs us of our joy and sets unrealistic standards for what we believe we are owed.

Comparison quickly breeds envy, jealousy, anxiety, and inadequacy if we don't identify and eliminate it. It distracts us from the job God has given us to do and the people He has called us to love.

One way we fight against comparison is by rooting for our rivals. You want to take the pressure of toxic competition out of your life? Start praying for your friends and the girls in your class. As soon as you start to hear comparison's tricky voice whispering in your ear that someone is better at something than you are, stop and ask God to bless her abundantly.

> Father, sometimes it's easy to see someone else's success as my failure or to see someone's failure as my success. But neither of these choices brings You glory. Help me root for others. Amen.

MEAN GIRLS

"I say to you who hear Me, love those who work against you. Do good to those who hate you. Respect and give thanks for those who try to bring bad to you. Pray for those who make it very hard for you."
LUKE 6:27–28

We've all known some mean girls. The relentless judgment and scrutiny by a ringleader and her friends can lead to worry and unease, always anticipating criticism or exclusion—which can become its own type of social anxiety.

So what do we do about it?

First, to be clear, *never* put yourself in harm's way. If someone is threatening or bullying you, or you are afraid for your safety, always tell a trusted adult.

But understand this: hurtful words or actions from mean girls are always a reflection of their own insecurities. Surround yourself with good friends who will help you respond calmly but confidently, and set boundaries that will keep you safe.

And never allow a mean girl to influence your way of thinking about yourself or others. God's words should always be the loudest words in your ears.

Father, please help me resist the temptation to retaliate or stoop to the level of unkind girls. Instead, give me strength and wisdom to lead by example and demonstrate the love that You have shown to me. Amen.

THRILL RIDE

Whatever work you do, do it with all your heart. Do it for the Lord and not for men.
COLOSSIANS 3:23

Let's talk about the immense pressure to perform. When the fear of failing at our goals, disappointing others, or being judged becomes the loudest voice in our heads, we are drowning in the pressure of performance.

It's important to understand that our worth and worthiness have nothing to do with our achievements. Otherwise we'll constantly ride the roller coaster of accomplishment and value.

When I look back on my teenage years, one of my biggest regrets is looking for validation in my accomplishments. When I was winning, I was worthy—and when I wasn't... *I wasn't*. And pressure on teenage girls today is far greater than when I was a teen.

One way we combat value-driven performance is by setting realistic goals. Setting the right goals is both a skill and a recipe for hope.

In the next few pages, we'll look at three specific areas in which you may be feeling unrelenting pressure to perform: academics, extracurricular activities, and friends.

Remember this: you can never be more loved than you already are.

Father, help me to remember that my worth is not found in my achievements, and my value doesn't lie in what I do but in who You made me to be. Amen.

PERFECTION PARALYSIS

Everyone should look at himself and see how he does his own work. Then he can be happy in what he has done. He should not compare himself with his neighbor. Everyone must do his own work.
GALATIANS 6:4–5

First, let's talk about pressure to excel at academics.

There is a fine line between *excellence* and *perfection*. And often it can be hard for outsiders looking in to distinguish the two since the outcomes look the same.

But one is helpful; one is not.

One gives life; one drains.

Excellence is the pursuit of our personal best. It requires us to grow and learn, but it allows for mistakes and celebrates improvement. Perfection, on the other hand, is an unattainable standard—a constantly moving target—filled with rigid expectations and a paralyzing fear of failure. Perfection can often look like constant self-criticism, stress, and anxiety. With perfection, our best is never enough.

Excellence strives for progress. Perfection is obsessed with flawlessness at all costs.

So, if the outcomes look similar, why does it matter? Answer: Excellence is for God. Perfection is for self. Excellence fosters joy, but perfection robs us of contentment.

Father, I know my job isn't to be perfect in my academics. My job is to do my best for Your glory. Please help me with this. Amen.

THE STRESS FACTOR

*So if you eat or drink or whatever you
do, do everything to honor God.*
1 CORINTHIANS 10:31

Now let's talk about pressure to excel at extracurricular activities.

Whether it's sports, arts, clubs, or music, the drive to achieve and stand out among your peers can be overwhelming. You may feel like you need to juggle numerous activities at the expense of free time or rest. And the fear of falling behind in any of these pursuits or missing out on opportunities that could improve your future can create chronic stress.

Two questions: Are you losing sleep because of your participation in extracurricular activities? Are you currently participating in any activities you don't enjoy simply because you believe they will make you look good? If either or both of these are true, they could be the cause of some anxiety.

If done correctly and with the right motive, sports, music, and art can become a positive outlet for stress. But if done simply to impress others, they have every ability to make life worse.

If you can't participate in extracurricular activities without feeling immense pressure to perform or excel, it may be time to have an honest conversation with your parents or teachers about the risk and reward.

> Father, thank You for the good gift
> of extracurricular activities. Help me
> prioritize them correctly. Amen.

QUALITY, NOT QUANTITY

Everything you do should be done in love.
1 CORINTHIANS 16:14

Finally, let's talk about pressure to excel socially.

Teen girls, especially, can feel the need to be *all the things*: outgoing, popular, funny. But none of these are expectations given to us in scripture, and none of them come with any guarantee of happiness or long-term fulfillment. In fact, popularity comes with its own price. Popularity can attract people who are only interested in the perceived benefits of association rather than genuinely taking interest in the popular person.

Many of the world's most popular people are also some of the loneliest.

It's a myth that being popular will make you happy. We are happiest when we are living the life and using the gifts God has given *us* to please *Him*.

Truly excelling socially comes with nurturing meaningful connections rather than chasing superficial acceptance. And how do we create meaningful connection? We learn to truly care about others as much or more than we care about ourselves. We ask genuine, curious questions about their lives and interests, and then we listen to their answers.

Research continues to show that it isn't the number of our friends but the quality of our friendships that actually matters most.

> Father, please help me prioritize quality friendships. And then help me love them as You love them. Amen.

IDENTITY THEFT

We all make many mistakes. If anyone does not make a mistake with his tongue by saying the wrong things, he is a perfect man. It shows he is able to make his body do what he wants it to do.
JAMES 3:2

Anxiety often looks like perfectionism in girls: high standards, fear of failure, self-criticism, excessive planning, mental or emotional distress.

Only God is required to be perfect. *I know, rocket science, right?* But how often do we live like we want to be perfect too?

As humans we make mistakes, have limitations, and grow through trial and error. We are flawed, and that cannot be changed this side of heaven. And honestly, flawed people want to connect authentically with other flawed people. The need for perfection and control is actually very isolating.

Recognizing—and accepting—that perfection is an attribute that belongs only to God frees us from the burden of unrealistic (and ultimately unmet) expectations. Understanding that we will never reach perfectionism in our lifetime enables us to focus on the better goals of growth and godliness.

> Father, if I learn to find my identity in You instead of my achievement, I won't be defined by my best or worst days. Neither will I be the sum of my achievements or failures. Help me learn this way of living. Amen.

IMPORTANT TO NOTE

Remember that you will get your reward from the Lord. He will give you what you should receive. You are working for the Lord Christ.
COLOSSIANS 3:24

You don't need to *be* the best at everything you do; you simply need to *do* your best. This is an important distinction in every area of life.

Typically speaking, if we're trying to please God with our effort, we won't fall into the trap of perfectionism. It's when we're comparing ourselves or trying to outshine everyone around us that we make the mistake of aiming for perfection.

Give yourself permission to let go of this unhelpful pressure. It's okay—*more than okay*—to have strengths in certain areas and not in others. *You aren't God.* Learn to set achievable, realistic goals that emphasize growth and improvement rather than unattainable, shifting standards. Celebrate small victories and accept limitations along the way.

Recognizing what you're good at doing is actually a helpful skill when planning your future. And embracing your strengths and weaknesses gives you permission to better appreciate your progress and celebrate the success of others without feeling inadequate because of it.

Remember, letting go of perfectionism is a process that takes time and patience, but it's absolutely worth the work.

> Father, please help me to remember that You are God and I am not. I want to please You most of all. Amen.

HOW TO BE A MUCH-LOVED DAUGHTER

"The mountains may be taken away and the hills may shake, but My loving-kindness will not be taken from you. And My agreement of peace will not be shaken," says the Lord who has loving-pity on you.
ISAIAH 54:10

Hear me carefully. You don't have to perform to be loved. If you are loved because of your achievements, that is not actually love. Remember these things:

You are not a fraud.

You are not a mistake.

You are worth the work to figure this out.

We'll look closer at each of those ideas, but first: One of my favorite stories in the Bible is when Jesus was baptized. He came up out of the water, and the Spirit of God came down and rested on Him like a dove. And then the voice of God said, "This is My much-loved Son. I am very happy with Him" (Matthew 3:17). One of the reasons I love these words so much is because Jesus hadn't yet performed any of His famous miracles.

God didn't love Jesus for His *accomplishments*. God loved Jesus for His *obedience*.

This is His desire for you: be a child of God who obeys. Faithfulness, commitment, and obedience are worth more than mere external achievement or temporary success.

> Father, I want to please You in all I do. Help me to want obedience more than accomplishment. Amen.

BEHIND THE SMILE

God's Law has power over my mind, but sin still has power over my sinful old self. I thank God I can be free through Jesus Christ our Lord!
ROMANS 7:25

....

Battling anxiety or depression doesn't make you a *fraud*. It makes you *human*.

Keep in mind: every single person in the world battles something. A relatable quote that has been attributed to many different people says, "Everyone you meet is fighting a battle you know nothing about."

Everyone's battle may not be obvious—especially for the girl at school who looks like she has it all together. She may even tell you she has no worries or weaknesses and that life is perfect.

The mirage of social media can convince us that everyone else's life is easy and ours is the only one with problems. But behind every person's smile is a hidden struggle or personal pain—physical, mental, emotional, or social. Nobody gets through this life without difficulty.

This knowledge should give you greater courage to be honest about your struggles, and it should equip you with deeper compassion for the people in your life.

> Father, I know nobody gets through life without a limp. Help me have compassion for those around me. Amen.

SISTER, YOU ARE NOT A MISTAKE

As for God, His way is perfect. The Word of the Lord has stood the test. He is a covering for all who go to Him for a safe place.
PSALM 18:30

You are not a mistake. We know this for sure because *God never makes mistakes.*

No matter the circumstances of your birth or life, your existence on this planet at this moment is neither random nor accidental. You are unique, gifted by God with a purpose and place in the world.

Nothing you ever do is outside the reaches of God's ability to use it for your good and His glory. We make mistakes; He doesn't.

Every experience, challenge, and setback in your life is shaping you into the person you are becoming. When you do or say something you regret, make it right and move on. Refuse to get stuck thinking about your mistakes. God's grace exists for you right here, today, where you are.

This world is better because you are in it. You are an irreplaceable part of God's grand design.

Just because you battle anxiety or depression doesn't mean you are a mistake. Do your best, ask for help when you need it, and trust that God will work everything according to His plan.

> Father, thank You for the confidence that I am here by Your design. Amen.

NOTE TO THE TRY-HARD GIRL

"Look at the birds in the sky. They do not plant seeds. They do not gather grain. They do not put grain into a building to keep. Yet your Father in heaven feeds them! Are you not more important than the birds?"
Matthew 6:26

You are worth the work to figure this out.

As we've seen, God's love for you is not based on your skills or achievements. It is only and always based on your inherent worth and value, created in you by God and secured for you by Jesus.

Romans 5:8 says, "God showed His love to us. While we were still sinners, Christ died for us." Before you ever did anything of value for God or for anybody else—before you were even born—*Jesus loved you*.

This truth should be unspeakable comfort for the try-hard girl. There is nothing you can do to be more loved and nothing you can do to be less loved by God. And one of the greatest ways you can show your gratitude for this kind of love is by accepting it without performance.

Our insecurity is always an invitation from God to escape the danger of false beliefs about who we are without Jesus.

> Father, thank You for loving me. When I am insecure, help me to remember to lean into You. Amen.

WHO DO YOU THINK YOU ARE?

We are His work. He has made us to belong to Christ Jesus so we can work for Him. He planned that we should do this.
Ephesians 2:10

If we're not crystal clear about our identity, we'll spend our entire lives either being swept away in a sea of inspirational Pinterest quotes or shape-shifting to be like whomever we currently want acceptance from. And God intends *so much more* for our lives than all of that.

So who does God say that you are?

You were a good idea in the mind of God even before He made the world. You were a masterpiece, carefully crafted in His divine plan. Before He made the world, He envisioned your worth, purpose, and potential. And now you are an image bearer, made for His glory.

Could there be anything better?

Often when we struggle with anxiety, it's because we've lost sight of who God is and who He made us to be. And our problems become bigger to us than the one who is committed to solving them with and for us.

If you come away from this book with only one thing, I hope you are secure in God's love for and acceptance of you.

> Father, there are so many distractions in my life. Help me keep my heart and mind fixed on You. Amen.

A QUESTION WORTH ASKING

Let your minds and hearts be made new.
EPHESIANS 4:23

This is one of the oldest and most frequently asked questions in the world: *Can people change?*

And the answer: yes! Not only does the Bible tell us that God is able and committed to helping us change to become more like Jesus but also that He created us to be adaptable creatures—capable of growth and transformation.

Fear and anxiety may be your battle to fight through life—*we never reach a point in life where we don't have challenges*—but you do not need to be controlled by fear or sadness.

Change can be challenging. But through the tools outlined for you in this book, you can begin to shift your perspective, change your behavior, and improve your habits. It will require effort, patience, and an unwavering commitment to truth. But with God's help and the help of people He has placed (or will place) in your life, victory is possible.

Here's what I know for sure: God can solve whatever challenges we have—and He has given us exactly what we need to do it.

In the following devotions, we will talk about three of the best tools God has given us for this fight.

> Father, please help me to remember that—
> in every battle—You are my ultimate
> source of strength and victory. Amen.

A LIVING BOOK

Your Word is a lamp to my feet and a light to my path.
PSALM 119:105

The first tool God has given us in our fight against anxiety and depression: *scripture*.

No other book in the world is alive (Hebrews 4:12). The wisdom found in its pages provides comfort in times of despair, guidance in moments of uncertainty, and strength in seasons of weakness.

Every time you read your Bible, you read holy and inspired words meant to transform your life.

You may not be a reader. If you struggle to read your Bible consistently because you don't enjoy reading, I encourage you to download an app—with your parents' permission—that enables you to listen to God's Word.

A few years ago, I experienced a very difficult season in my life, and I found it hard to concentrate on reading anything of value. But I knew it was important that I read my Bible. So, on the days when I couldn't read, I would play Psalm 23 and just let the words fill my heart and mind. And those words brought me greater comfort and peace than anything else ever could.

> Father, thank You for the priceless treasure of Your Word. Thank You for revealing Yourself to me through its pages. Help me love it, study it, and allow it to transform my life. Amen.

NOTE(S) TO SELF

*He finds joy in the Law of the Lord and
thinks about His Law day and night.*
Psalm 1:2

We talked in the preceding devotion about the tool of scripture. Here's an important and practical way to use that tool in your daily life: find verses that specifically address your greatest needs and put them in places where you know you'll see them when you need them.

When I was a teenager, my mom printed 1 Corinthians 10:13 on a sheet of neon-pink printer paper and posted it inside my closet. Though it's a long verse ("You have never been tempted to sin in any different way than other people. God is faithful. He will not allow you to be tempted more than you can take. But when you are tempted, He will make a way for you to keep from falling into sin"), it was easy to memorize because I saw it every time I opened my closet door. It was also helpful to me when I was met with overwhelming temptation or when I believed there was no way out.

On index cards or sticky notes, write out verses and put them on your bedroom mirror, in your planner, in your locker at school—wherever you will see the verses and be reminded of truth.

Biblical truth is your greatest weapon in the fight against the lies of the enemy.

> Father, please help me never take for granted the privilege of having access to Your words and will for my life in the Bible. Amen.

LIFELINE

Be happy in your hope. Do not give up when trouble comes. Do not let anything stop you from praying.
ROMANS 12:12

We know that God has given us the tool of *scripture* to fight anxiety and depression, but He has also given us the tool of *prayer*.

Think of it this way: The great God of the universe—your Creator—has given you an invitation to talk to Him about anything. Nothing is too big or too small to discuss with God.

Recently, I heard a young woman—I believe well-meaning—say that we should stop telling people with anxiety and depression to pray as a means of fighting it. While I agree we shouldn't tell people that prayer is the only way to fight anxiety and depression, I think it would be a horrible mistake to leave prayer out of the battle.

While I'm absolutely in favor of pursuing many tools (anxiety and depression are complex, and so are humans!), I can't overlook prayer, for that is God's remedy. *Don't let anything stop you from praying.*

Philippians 4:6, "Do not worry. Learn to pray about everything. Give thanks to God as you ask Him for what you need," isn't a random to-do list—it's a problem and a solution. Want to fight worry? Learn to pray about everything.

Father, thank You for the privilege of talking directly to You and knowing You will hear me. Amen.

GROUNDED

Never stop praying.
1 Thessalonians 5:17

Why is it that the easiest Bible verse to read or memorize is also one of the hardest verses to obey? "Never stop praying" takes two seconds to memorize and a lifetime to practice. Some Bible scholars believe prayer is the hardest discipline of the Christian life. But prayer is also our biggest need and greatest gift.

Never stop praying:

Even when it's hard to talk to God.

Even when a situation feels too hard to handle.

Even when previous prayers haven't been answered the way you would choose.

Even when you're tired.

Even when you're not completely convinced that God is listening.

Even when you don't know what to say.

Never ever stop praying.

Prayer enables us to surrender our worries, fears, and anxieties to God—who can carry them perfectly for us. By acknowledging to God in prayer what we need, we can receive the comfort and help that come only from Him.

Pray big prayers. Pray specific prayers. Pray frequent prayers.

Prayer will always be hard work, but it will always be the best work we do.

Father, You owe me nothing, yet You invite me to come to You with confidence, and You promise to hear and answer according to Your will. Thank You. Amen.

FIND YOUR PEOPLE

*Help each other in troubles and problems.
This is the kind of law Christ asks us to obey.*
GALATIANS 6:2

We've seen in the last few devotions that God has given us the tools of *scripture* and *prayer* to fight anxiety and depression, but He has also given us the tool of *community*.

Christian community is a gift meant to enrich our lives in countless ways. In addition to providing a sense of belonging and support, good friends and godly mentors offer biblical perspectives that point us to truth when we're struggling to see it.

Whether you're an introvert or an extrovert, God intends for community to be a good gift in your life.

The right kind of friends and mentors will have the courage to speak the truth even when it may be difficult to hear. They will offer sincere guidance, constructive criticism, and honest perspectives—driven by a genuine desire for your growth and well-being.

Good friends and mentors help us identify blind spots and point us to lasting truth over momentary comfort. If you find friends and mentors who have the courage to be truthful, hold on to them. Friends who love Jesus and pursue truth are worth holding on to.

Father, thank You for the good gift of community.
You designed me to live in fellowship with
other believers for the purpose of support and
encouragement. Help me embrace it. Amen.

TAKE FIVE

Plans go wrong without talking together, but they will go well when many wise men talk about what to do.
PROVERBS 15:22

Who are five safe, trusted people in your life?

Five is not a magical number. You may have lots of trusted people—if so, great! But the important thing is that you *have* a few safe, trusted people. You want more than one, but you don't want so many that it's hard to foster good relationships.

Ideally, at least three of your safe, trusted people should be adults that you can trust—a parent, a teacher, a leader in your youth group at church. Can you name these people? If not, this is a new and healthy goal to work toward.

These five safe, trusted people are not necessarily the same kids you might hang out with at school. These should be people you would go to for advice or when struggling with a challenge.

By investing your time and energy in five safe, trusted people, you can cultivate closer relationships built on trust, loyalty, and mutual honesty.

You want these safe, trusted people to be wise, honest, and God-loving. But it shouldn't just be about what they can do for you. You should want to love and respect them enough to be a benefit in their lives as well.

> Father, please show me who I should pursue as my closest relationships. Amen.

YOUR MOVE

*A man who has friends must be a friend, but there
is a friend who stays nearer than a brother.*
PROVERBS 18:24

Maybe in evaluating who your people are, you realize that you need to have better friends.

May I make a recommendation? If you need better friends, *you* make the first move. You have everything you need to lead the way.

What teenage girl in your church or school is someone you admire for her good choices or authentic joy? Who is someone you know to be kind and reliable? Who do you know who authentically loves Jesus?

Instead of just looking for someone who has a lot in common with you—favorite books, movies, or hobbies—what if you looked for a friend who would be *good for you*... someone who would point you to Christ and encourage you to be a healthier version of who He made you to be?

Change in any area is hard, but especially when it comes to our friendships. Thankfully, building mutually beneficial relationships with the right people is one of the best things we can do with our time and attention. The benefits truly are endless.

> Father, would You help me find a good friend? Would You also prepare me to be a good friend as well? Amen.

TELL THE TRUTH

If we say that we have no sin, we lie to ourselves and the truth is not in us. If we tell Him our sins, He is faithful and we can depend on Him to forgive us of our sins. He will make our lives clean from all sin.
1 John 1:8–9

We know God has given us tools to fight our anxiety and depression—including *scripture*, *prayer*, and *community*. But finally, He has given us the tool of *truth telling*.

We talked in an earlier devotion about how deeply important truth is in our battle against anxiety and depression. There is great power in simply being honest—the Bible tells us that truth makes us free (John 8:32). Free from what?—the bondage of fear, hopelessness, and anxiety.

Truth telling is foundational to building trust. When you consistently speak the truth, others can rely on your words and actions, and trust is built. Truth telling is also essential for building relationships and resolving conflicts.

But more than that, truth brings lies and deceptions into the light. It exposes hidden agendas and disrupts unhealthy or unhelpful systems.

We should speak and seek the truth at all times.

Specifically, it's important to be honest with yourself, honest with your parents, and honest with God. Let's look briefly at each of those in the next few devotions.

> Father, please give me the courage
> to tell the truth always. Amen.

TALK TO YOURSELF

See, You want truth deep within the heart. And You will make me know wisdom in the hidden part.
PSALM 51:6

It's important to be honest with yourself. That should be easy, right? Not necessarily.

Being honest with ourselves requires us to challenge our own thoughts and perceptions, which can be uncomfortable. Our own sinful ego would prefer to resist the truth, clinging instead to comfortable illusions and time-tested rationalizations.

So, what does being honest with ourselves look like? We learn to ask questions such as these: *Is this really true? Does what I'm saying or believing line up with what God says in His Word? Is this actually what I believe or just what I want people to think I believe?*

Being honest with ourselves is a lifelong process. Learning to speak truth to ourselves requires courage, vulnerability, and a commitment to please God.

Unfortunately, you can't make anyone be honest with you, but you get to decide what you say to yourself. You get to choose the words, thoughts, and beliefs that you internalize and repeat, especially when you're alone with your thoughts.

Father, would You show me areas in my life where I have been deceiving myself or living in denial? I want to be truthful with myself. Amen.

LET'S DO SOME DIGGING

*"Nothing is secret but what will be known.
Anything that is hidden will be brought into the light."*
LUKE 8:17

Once you are being honest with yourself, you can more easily identify where the anxiety or depression is coming from.

Maybe your anxiety is coming from unrealistic expectations or the fear of rejection. Maybe you're struggling to adjust to something new or you're comparing your life to somebody else's and wishing you could have different circumstances.

It makes sense that identifying where the fear, anxiety, or depression is coming from would be a good step in being able to address it.

If—even being honest with yourself—you find it hard to identify what is causing your anxiety or depression, talk to the safe, trusted people in your life. Your parents or mentors may already have some good thoughts. Ask them this question: "What do you see in my life that could be causing my anxiety?"

Multiple things could be contributing to your battle. Be ready to hear what your trusted friends or mentors have to say. It may surprise you. Even better, *it may help*.

> Father, please give me the strength to face any hidden fears, insecurities, or past wounds that may contribute to my anxiety. Amen.

THE BEAUTIFUL TRUTH

He who speaks the truth tells what is right, but a liar tells lies.
PROVERBS 12:17

I'm going to assume that your parents—*though imperfect, because we all are imperfect people*—love you and want what's best for you. In the event that this isn't your story and you do not have a healthy relationship with one or both of your parents, please simply substitute "responsible adult in your life" for "parent" in these pages.

As females, we typically know what we're expected to say and do, especially at home. We know the right answers—even if we don't always agree with them. This can sometimes lead to dishonesty because we want to earn our parents' approval or maintain a sense of calm at home.

But in addition to being honest with yourself, you need to be honest with your parents. Being honest is essential for healthy communication and trust building, especially in the teen years. Honesty at home invites your parents to provide the support and guidance you need.

Whatever challenges you face, your parents likely are able to help. But they can only offer the support you need if you're honest with them about the difficulties you're facing.

You may be surprised by how willing they are to listen and help if you tell them the truth.

> Father, give me the courage to tell my parents what I am feeling or facing, believing they have my best interests in mind. Amen.

WHEN HOME IS HARD

*I will be careful to live a life without blame.
When will You come to me? I will walk within
my house with a right and good heart.*
PSALM 101:2

What should you do when your anxiety is caused by what's happening at home?

No home is immune to sinful and destructive patterns of speech or behavior. Even in Christian homes, parents or children set unreasonable expectations for each other and say cruel and ungodly things.

Again, I'm not talking about abuse here. If you are afraid for your safety, always tell a trusted adult. But what can you do about general, daily sinful behavior?

First, understand that where you live is not a mistake. God loves you and sees what's happening in the walls of your home.

Second, if at all possible—and at a time when tempers aren't already high—seek to talk to your parents in a way that is honoring but honest.

In 1 Peter 2:23, Jesus gave us the ultimate example of how to respond. "When people spoke against Him, He never spoke back. When He suffered from what people did to Him, He did not try to pay them back. He left it in the hands of the One Who is always right in judging."

> Father, when things are hard at home,
> I trust You to judge rightly. Amen.

A CALL FOR COURAGE

My children, let us not love with words or in talk only. Let us love by what we do and in truth.
1 JOHN 3:18

In addition to being honest with yourself and your parents, it's important for you to be honest with your friends.

Think carefully for a minute. Do you ever agree to do something you really don't want to do? Do you ever change your mind or opinion about something important simply because your friends think differently about an issue?

Girls sometimes confuse *being accommodating* with *being kind*. But honesty isn't just the absence of lies—it's also the presence of truth. If you think differently about an issue or an idea but you pretend you agree with the group, that isn't honest.

Being honest means others can rely on our words and actions. Being honest helps us avoid misunderstandings and conflicts. Telling the truth enables clarity and resolves issues before they escalate.

When we're truthful with our friends—in a loving but uncompromising way—we invite them to do the same with us. And the healthiest friendships flourish in honesty. It makes sense, then, why 1 John 3:18 says that telling the truth is one way we love the people in our lives.

> Father, please give me the courage to speak openly and honestly with my friends while being kind and glorifying You. Amen.

A PLACE TO BELONG

You belong to Christ, and Christ belongs to God.
1 CORINTHIANS 3:23

One of our deepest human needs is to belong.

Human beings long for social connection and companionship. Belonging satisfies our deep need for acceptance, support, and emotional connection. Belonging provides us with a sense of identity and purpose. When we belong to a group who shares our values, traditions, and goals, we feel a sense of safety and security.

The opposite of belonging—when we don't feel like we're part of a community—leads us to feeling isolated and vulnerable. When we feel set outside a group or community, we often feel unacknowledged or unappreciated. And isolation is a terrible feeling.

But belonging to the right group makes all the difference.

If your current friend group will only accept you if you agree with them or bend to their demands or expectations of you, do you truly belong?

You belong to Christ. You are more deeply loved and accepted than you could ever begin to imagine. And by extension, you belong to the body of Christ, His church. If you have a habit of changing yourself to fit into a group, consider looking for different friendships and acceptance.

> Father, please help me keep looking until I find true and lasting belonging with people who want to please You. Amen.

HONEST TO GOD

Even before I speak a word, O Lord, You know it all.
PSALM 139:4

In addition to being honest with yourself, your parents, and your friends, it's important to be honest with God. People flippantly throw around the phrase "honest to God," but few people are actually *honest to God*.

Yes, God is omniscient—meaning He already knows everything. But by being honest with Him, we acknowledge and accept who He is and who we are. Throughout the Bible, we are invited—even commanded—to tell God the truth. "Trust in Him at all times, O people. Pour out your heart before Him. God is a safe place for us" (Psalm 62:8).

Dishonesty in any form—to ourselves, to our parents, to our friends, or to God—is most often the result of pride. And God wants us to humble ourselves in His presence.

Honesty with God cultivates trust and surrender. When we bring God our sorrows, successes, and failures—surrendering them to Him with open hands and tender hearts—we place our trust in His wisdom and plan for our lives.

None of this happens if we remain unwilling to be honest with our good and gracious God.

> Father, please help me always acknowledge my doubts, fears, and struggles to You. You know them already and love me anyway. Amen.

GRUMBLE-FREE ZONE

You must have faith as you ask Him. You must not doubt. Anyone who doubts is like a wave which is pushed around by the sea.
JAMES 1:6

One practical thought on being honest with God: watch the way you talk to Him.

By that I mean, if your prayers aren't filled with gratitude for who God is and what He has done, you may be inadvertently using prayer to reinforce fear and anxiety.

Yes, be honest with God. Of course, be honest with God! What's the point of praying if we don't tell the truth? But our prayers shouldn't just be lists of fears or complaints. They should also be thoughtful opportunities to praise God for who He is and what He can do about our situation. Our prayers should be filled with God's truth, not just our unhappiness.

Yes, David, the writer of many psalms, poured out his fears and anxieties to God—and so should you—but David always turned his attention back to what he knew to be true about God. And often, David thanked God for answering his requests even before receiving anything in response to his prayers.

In the following devotions, let's look at three reasons we should bring anxiety—along with our gratitude—to God.

> Father, let my words and thoughts please You. Help me remember to whom I'm talking when I pray. Amen.

CAN GOD BE TRUSTED?

"You will keep the man in perfect peace whose mind is kept on You, because he trusts in You."
ISAIAH 26:3

The first reason we should bring the anxiety we face—along with our gratitude—to God is because He is *trustworthy*. Two thoughts: *First, how and whom we trust is never neutral.* Trust always involves being vulnerable and taking risks. The level of trust we place in someone or something depends on how greatly we view the risks involved. If we believe God is not trustworthy, we'll be cautious and slow to trust Him.

Second, how and whom we trust always changes us from the inside out. In this case, we can trust God completely because He has proven Himself to be fully trustworthy. Throughout history, God has proven Himself to be all-knowing, all-powerful, and completely good. So even when His plans don't make sense, we can trust that He won't fail us either.

Building the muscle of trust takes work, but if we're willing to trust only when we have all the answers we want and need, we're not actually trusting God, but ourselves.

> Father, I humble myself in Your presence, acknowledging that You are God and I am not. You are my Father, and You can do me no wrong. Help me trust You. Amen.

NEVER FOR NOTHING

We know that God makes all things work together for the good of those who love Him and are chosen to be a part of His plan.
ROMANS 8:28

The second reason we should bring our anxiety—along with our gratitude—to God: He can redeem *anything*.

Either in this life or in the next, God can and will redeem every hard thing you've experienced. That relationship that fell apart? Those fears you can't seem to control? Those mistakes from your past that haunt you at night? None of it is outside His reach.

Through redemption, God invites us to let go of hard or hurtful situations where the outcomes weren't what we'd hoped, and He invites us to trust His ability to rewrite the narrative for our good and for His glory.

In Romans 8:28, God specifically pledged to make the painful events in your life have meaning and purpose. He is that good and kind.

The most beautiful stories are often the ones where someone suffered profoundly and still found God to be faithful and true—even while suffering.

So, if you're struggling, keep trusting. God isn't done writing your story until it's entirely *good*.

Father, in my moments of doubt or confusion, please help me to hold steadfastly to Your promises. Remind me of Your faithfulness throughout history and in my own life. Amen.

GOOD GIFTS

Whatever is good and perfect comes to us from God. He is the One Who made all light. He does not change. No shadow is made by His turning.
JAMES 1:17

. . . .

The third reason we should bring our anxiety—along with our gratitude—to God is because He gives good gifts. He *wants* to give you good gifts when you're struggling.

Some of His good gifts to us when we're battling anxiety include comfort, hope, strength, community, and wisdom.

In Philippians 4, Paul said that when we come to God in prayer—making our requests and thanksgiving known to Him—He gives us His peace that passes our human understanding. And isn't His peace what we most want and need when we're anxious?

In 2 Corinthians 12, Paul said that God's power is made perfect when we are weak. And don't we feel weak when we're battling anxiety?

Everything good in your life comes to you from your God who is good. He is your good Father who wants to give you good gifts. So it is only logical and right that we learn to bring our anxiety to Him. He can help us with it.

Next, let's talk more about two of God's good gifts that specifically help us when we're battling anxiety or depression.

Father, please help me recognize and appreciate the good gifts You give me every day. Amen.

THE ROAD NOT TAKEN

I receive joy when I am weak. I receive joy when people talk against me and make it hard for me and try to hurt me and make trouble for me. I receive joy when all these things come to me because of Christ. For when I am weak, then I am strong.
2 CORINTHIANS 12:10

One of God's good gifts to us: grace. His grace is always there for us when we need it, but it isn't necessarily there for what-ifs.

Said another way, God isn't obligated to give us grace for the scary scenarios we create in our imaginations. He gives grace when we're truly in a moment of need. The what-ifs can haunt our thoughts and steal our peace. They can create horrible scenarios that may never come to pass.

What if I had made a different choice?
What if things don't work out as planned?
What if I fail?

These questions can be paralyzing, keeping us trapped in endless cycles of doubt and fear. And they can rob us of the joy found in this present moment. God's grace exists for us in real life *right now*.

And in the rare event that the worst case actually happens, God's grace will meet us there too.

> Father, thank You for Your grace, available in abundance for the choices I make and actions I take today. Amen.

THE GOD WHO SEES

For I know that nothing can keep us from the love of God. Death cannot! Life cannot! Angels cannot! Leaders cannot! Any other power cannot! Hard things now or in the future cannot! The world above or the world below cannot! Any other living thing cannot keep us away from the love of God which is ours through Christ Jesus our Lord.
ROMANS 8:38–39

Another of God's good gifts to us: His presence.

God promises to be with us no matter what! In the face of chaos and confusion, God doesn't just watch from a distance, wondering how things will turn out or if we'll be okay. He experiences life *with* us. The Creator of the universe—our Creator—holds our hands and quiets our hearts.

And still, we might be tempted to say—as Gideon did in Judges 6:13—"If the Lord is with us, why has all this happened to us?"

We don't have all the answers to the hard questions in our lives, but we can learn to ask better questions. *What can I learn about God from this situation? Where do I see His faithfulness in my life today?*

> God, all throughout the Bible, You promise me Your presence. If I want anything here on earth more than I want Your presence, help me to see and change my priority. Amen.

ALL LIES

"The devil is your father. You are from him. You want to do the sinful things your father, the devil, wants you to do. He has been a killer from the beginning. The devil has nothing to do with the truth. There is no truth in him. It is expected of the devil to lie, for he is a liar and the father of lies."
JOHN 8:44

We need to *notice the lies*.

As in, Satan is the father of lies, and he's really good at telling them. Good lies are eerily similar to truth, which can make them harder to identify and easier to believe.

Lies obscure the truth and distort reality. They look like misinformation, manipulation, and deceit. They create confusion and breed mistrust. They promise easy answers and instant gratification. But beneath their enticing exterior, they carry a heavy price.

Believing lies can erode our relationships, fracture our families, and create division. We have to notice the places where we're tempted to believe things that are inconsistent with what God says is true. Here are some good examples of lies you may be tempted to believe:

If I have more friends, I'll be happy.
What I look like determines what I'm worth.
I'm completely in control of my life.

> Father, please give me strength to resist the enemy's temptations, to reject his lies, and to choose obedience to You no matter what. Amen.

ANXIETY IS A LIAR

"See, I go east, but He is not there. I go west, but I cannot see Him. When He works to the left, I cannot see Him. When He turns to the right, I cannot see Him."
Job 23:8–9

Speaking of lies, anxiety is a liar.

Here are three things anxiety often lies about:

Anxiety lies about our safety. Often, anxiety exaggerates our level of threat or danger. It leads us to believe a small uncertainty is actually a catastrophic event waiting to happen. It amplifies our fears and quiets our certainties. Anxiety is happiest when we feel unsafe.

Anxiety lies about our ability. With God, we can meet our responsibilities in His strength, but anxiety likes to convince us that we are incompetent. Anxiety seeks to undermine what God has done for us in the past and what He can do for us in the future. Anxiety is happiest when we feel incapable.

Anxiety lies about our future. Anxiety tells us we are destined for failure and that we can't overcome our current challenges. It traps us in a frustrating cycle of negative expectations and unhelpful limitations. Anxiety is happiest when we are stuck in the past.

> Father, anxiety knows nothing of Your love or goodness. Help me choose to listen to You instead of to fear and anxiety. Amen.

DEPRESSION IS A LIAR

*Let the peace of Christ have power over your hearts.
You were chosen as a part of His body. Always be thankful.*
COLOSSIANS 3:15

Not only is anxiety a liar, but depression is a liar.

Depression has a way of distorting our thoughts and perceptions, leading us away from truth. Here are some things depression lies about:

You are alone, and nobody cares about you.
You are worthless, and you have no purpose.
Things will never get better.
You are the one to blame for every bad thing that has happened to you.

But here is what I most want you to understand: Those dark whispers in your mind are not the reality of who you are or what your future holds. Not even close.

These lies come directly from the enemy, who still whispers lies just like he did in the garden of Eden, asking us if we are sure of what we know. Are we sure God's promises are true? Are we sure God meant what He said?

If you've started believing things that aren't true about your life, start retelling your story to yourself until you believe it. You are not alone. You have worth and purpose. Things will get better. You are only responsible for your own choices.

> Father, please help me to constantly and vigilantly compare what I believe against what You say is true. Amen.

TWO TRUTHS AND A LIE

*Let the joy of Your saving power return to me.
And give me a willing spirit to obey You.*
PSALM 51:12

Not only do anxiety and depression tell lies, but they want you to avoid truths.

For example, anxiety and depression don't want you to know that *you have agency*. *Agency* is your ability to make choices that contribute to positive change. You are not at the mercy of anxiety or depression.

Anxiety and depression don't want you to know that *uncertainty is okay.* It's more than okay—it's part of life! Learning to accept that life is full of surprises can be very liberating.

Anxiety and depression don't want you to know that *human connection is helpful.* You don't have to wait until you "fix" your feelings before you connect with other people. In fact, you shouldn't wait until you feel better. Community is one of God's great gifts to help us manage anxiety.

And two of the most important truths that anxiety and depression don't want you to know: you are loved, and it's going to be okay.

Let's look more specifically at these two promises in the next two devotions.

> Father, please help me identify and overcome anxiety's deceitful whispers. Amen.

THIS FIERCE LOVE

"The Lord your God is with you, a Powerful One Who wins the battle. He will have much joy over you. With His love He will give you new life. He will have joy over you with loud singing."
ZEPHANIAH 3:17

. . . .

The first truth anxiety does not want you to know is simply this: *you are loved.*

You couldn't do anything to be any more loved than you are right now. You don't have to perform to be loved by God. The God who made you and knows you better than you know yourself loves you better than anyone else ever could.

There's nothing you can do to lose God's love. *Nothing.*

And when we start to better understand the wild, deep love of God for us, it's hard to stay afraid. Fear arises when we feel separated or unknown, but when we understand we are loved by the one who will never leave us and who knows everything about us and our future, we'll better understand safety and belonging.

You are loved. You are loved. *You are loved.*

> Father, Your wild, deep love for me has changed my life and brought me into relationship with You. Thank You. Amen.

ANXIETY'S BEST KEPT SECRET

*The little troubles we suffer now for a short
time are making us ready for the great
things God is going to give us forever.*
2 CORINTHIANS 4:17

Not only does your anxiety or depression not want you to know that you are loved but it also doesn't want you to know that everything is going to be okay.

Even though things may feel really hard right now, everything truly is going to be okay. It's hard to see beyond the struggles and challenges you're currently facing, but this is just one chapter in your story. God has good things planned for your life. There are no throwaway people or plans in God's economy.

I'm not saying that everything will be okay today or even by the end of this book. Anxiety and depression can be complicated. But the God who made you is committed to writing a good story with your life. *He only writes good stories.*

Think back to another time when you thought you couldn't push through something difficult. You made it, didn't you? God helped you persevere then, and He can help you persevere now.

Keep going, friend. It really will be okay.

Father, please give me patience and help me trust Your timing as I wait for better days. Amen.

FACTS AND FEELINGS

Our heart may say that we have done wrong. But remember, God is greater than our heart. He knows everything.
1 John 3:20

Let's talk about feelings.

God made us with feelings—they are part of His good design. Feelings enable us to better connect and care for others. It's hard, for example, to "be happy with those who are happy [and]. . .sad with those who are sad" (Romans 12:15) without feelings. Feelings make us unique in God's creation.

But it's important to remember that we must always anchor our feelings to truth.

"How does this make me feel?" is never more important than "What does God say?" God's Word is always the ultimate truth in our lives.

Feelings are fertile ground for good questions. We shouldn't make feelings the enemy, nor should we allow them to decide our choices and behavior.

Let's discuss four feelings that make us more susceptible to anxiety or depression. Note: these feelings may not be responsible for your anxiety or depression, but they can certainly leave you susceptible to attack.

> Father, thank You for Your display of infinite creativity, as seen in Your design of human emotions. Help me respond to them correctly and trust You in everything. Amen.

SEEING RED

*If you are angry, do not let it become sin.
Get over your anger before the day is finished.*
EPHESIANS 4:26

Let's talk about anger.

Some researchers believe that anger and anxiety are the same emotion. Anger simply *explodes* where anxiety *implodes*.

You may not consider yourself someone who gets angry very often, but consider these scenarios. Do any of them sound familiar to you?

- If you suppress your fear or other emotions long enough, the anxiety starts to build up until there's an explosion of tension, often over something that surprises even you.
- Stressful situations can lead to fearing a loss of control. Sometimes that fear of losing control leads to getting angry as a way of regaining control or masking underlying fears.
- Tension or pressure you put on yourself to perform can lead to heightened states of anxiety that fuel frustration and irritability—especially if someone says or does anything unhelpful. Minor issues can trigger angry responses.

If anger is something you deal with regularly, ask God for help with this emotion.

> Father, in my moments of anger, please give me the wisdom to pause, reflect, and respond in a way that honors You. Amen.

FOOD FOR THOUGHT

*It is not good to eat much honey,
and looking for honor is not good.*
PROVERBS 25:27

Let's talk about hunger. Hunger can make us more susceptible to anxiety.

When you're hungry, your blood sugar fluctuates and can lead to imbalances that affect your mood and overall well-being. These fluctuations can lead to feelings of irritability, restlessness, and anxiety.

Also, hunger can impact the way we think. It can cloud our judgment and change the way we make decisions. It can make it harder for us to cope with stressful situations. It can lessen our energy and heighten the feelings that decrease our natural resistance to stress.

So it's important to prioritize regular, healthy, balanced meals that stabilize our blood sugar levels, support optimal brain function, and help us reduce our vulnerability to anxiety.

Is anxiety always the result of hunger? Of course not. But when we start to feel anxious, it's a good idea to stop and consider how long it's been since we've had a healthy meal or snack. Eating something healthy can be a quick and easy way to solve a problem before it gets out of control.

> Father, please help me make good choices that honor both my body and my soul. Give me wisdom to know when the solution is as simple as a healthy snack. Amen.

LORD OF THE OUTCAST

*"Do for other people what you would
like to have them do for you."*
LUKE 6:31

Let's talk about loneliness.

Loneliness is a horrible feeling that arises from the belief that we are isolated or unable to connect with others. Sometimes it's because people in general are unkind and unwelcoming. At other times, it's because we want the friendship or attention of one person unwilling to acknowledge us.

Here are a few ways to combat loneliness:

- *Reach out to others.* Who else in your life may also be lonely? Take the initiative to reach out and make connections. Engage in conversation, ask questions, and show genuine interest in getting to know others.
- *Strengthen your existing friendships.* Don't wait to be invited to someone's house. You can make plans or start meaningful discussions.
- *Volunteer in your church or community.* Connect with others who share your values and interests. One of the wisest ways we overcome loneliness is by investing in other people.

Remember: building connections takes time and effort. You can't just wait for people to want to build a friendship with you—you also must take the initiative to reach out to others.

Father, somebody in my life is waiting for a friend, and I can be that friend. Please help me find her. Amen.

THE SCIENCE OF SLEEP

"Come to Me, all of you who work and have heavy loads. I will give you rest. Follow My teachings and learn from Me. I am gentle and do not have pride. You will have rest for your souls. For My way of carrying a load is easy and My load is not heavy."
MATTHEW 11:28–30

Finally, let's talk about exhaustion.

When we are physically or mentally exhausted, our bodies and brains are vulnerable to stress and less equipped to cope. When we're tired, we experience increased sensitivity—meaning minor challenges can become big problems for us really fast.

God designed our bodies to need rest. Did you know that according to sleep experts, you as a teenager should be getting eight to ten hours of sleep every night?

Yes, I know that number may feel impossible. But consistently getting enough sleep is critically important for your mental, emotional, and physical health.

It would be better to enjoy fewer waking hours that are better quality than to experience more waking hours that are stressful and hard.

What can you cut to make time for more sleep?

Father, as the good Creator, You have ordained rest as an important part of my life. Please help me understand and honor the priority of rest in maintaining good health. Amen.

NIGHT SONG

He will not let your feet go out from under you.
He Who watches over you will not sleep.
PSALM 121:3

It's two in the morning and you can't sleep. You toss and turn. You adjust—and then readjust—your pillow. You throw the covers off and then pull them back on again. And you watch the minutes on your clock tick by. Maybe you have no idea why you can't sleep, or maybe you know exactly what's troubling you.

What do you do? The answer is both simple and hard: give it to God and go to sleep.

David, who wrote many of the psalms, understood what it was like to have a quiet mind even when life itself wasn't quiet at all. Whether he was being hunted by his enemies or sinking in his sorrow, he learned how to sleep beneath the promises of God.

The same God who never stopped caring for David also cares for you. He can be trusted to hold your anxieties while you rest. And rest is so important in the battle against anxiety.

So what should we do with anxiety at night? Give it to God and go to sleep.

> Father, David knew that daytime and nighttime are the same to You. Help me trust You to care for me while I sleep. Amen.

GUT CHECK

Those who know Your name will put their trust in You. For You, O Lord, have never left alone those who look for You.
PSALM 9:10

A word on gut feelings.

Gut feelings, also known as *intuition* or *instinct*, can be a great gift. Females, especially, are known for having strong perception that can help us navigate the world.

That said, gut feelings are not facts. And sometimes our gut feelings can be wrong. What we sometimes perceive as a *gut feeling* can actually be the voice of fear, manifesting as a heightened sensitivity to a perceived threat or danger that doesn't actually exist.

We can misinterpret butterflies in the stomach to mean impending doom. And then soon, we're unwilling to try anything new or exciting because we're afraid.

So, how do we tell the difference between a gut feeling and an unnecessary fear? First, we always maintain a conversation with God in prayer. "Never stop praying" (1 Thessalonians 5:17).

Second, we learn to consider the context of the situation, seeking a balanced perspective and looking carefully at other relevant information. What is the risk involved? What do trusted friends or mentors suggest? What could go *right*?

> Father, I know I should pay attention to the instincts You gave me for my safety, but help me to learn to trust You more than I trust my gut. Amen.

FACING FEARS

Our hope comes from God. May He fill you with joy and peace because of your trust in Him. May your hope grow stronger by the power of the Holy Spirit.
ROMANS 15:13

Let courage lead the way.

Courage is not the absence of fear or doubt; it's the willingness to move forward even before we feel the courage to act. Courage is the choice to trust what God has promised us and to step outside our comfort zone and face the challenge head-on, regardless of the fear we may feel in the moment.

In other words, don't wait for your feelings to change before you practice courage. If you wait to act until you feel like doing something, you may never actually do it.

Whether it's that new friendship you need to pursue or the honesty you need to have with yourself or someone else or the activity you need to quit to make time to rest—courage is yours for the taking.

You have everything you need today to do what God wants you to do.

By choosing to take the first step even before you feel like doing it, you will actually break free from the limitations created for you by fear.

> Father, please replace my fear with faith, my hesitation with hope, and my weakness with strength. Amen.

A WORD OF CAUTION

We have power over all these things through Jesus Who loves us so much.
ROMANS 8:37

One quick word of caution: watch the way you talk about anxiety and depression. The way we talk about our struggles holds tremendous power in shaping how we view their control in our lives.

For example, maybe you've been legitimately victimized—or maybe your anxiety and depression are largely the result of poor choices made for you by other people—but thinking of yourself as a victim is one of the worst things you can do. A victim mentality can subtly creep into our lives, whispering lies that undermine God's goodness and our ability to thrive.

A victim's identity can keep us trapped.

Here's the truth: you are not defined by your struggles, and you have everything you need from God to rise above them. This idea isn't meant to minimize your painful experiences. Again, like I said in this book's first devotion, I believe you. But I want you to find the freedom to live your life in a healthy, God-glorifying way no matter what you've experienced.

Watch the way you talk about your anxiety and depression. What you say about it can reinforce the identity associated with that behavior.

Father, because of You and what You have done for me, I don't have to be trapped by what others have done. Give me courage to move forward. Amen.

TAKING IT PERSONALLY

See what great love the Father has for us that He would call us His children. And that is what we are. For this reason the people of the world do not know who we are because they did not know Him.

1 John 3:1

The first reason you should watch the way you talk about anxiety and depression: you don't want to be defined by *any* struggle you're experiencing.

Sometimes we fall into the trap of allowing our struggles to become our identity. Suddenly, our struggles become the main thing we think about, worry about, or talk about. But that limits the freedom we were meant to experience through Christ. He didn't purchase our identity on the cross so that we would define ourselves by our anxiety.

You are so much more than your battle with anxiety.

One practical way we can keep from defining ourselves by our struggle: try to avoid using the phrase "*my* anxiety." Put as much distance between it and you as you can. Anxiety is not who you are; it's something you experience.

Anxiety is something you battle from time to time, but it isn't who you are as a whole. It's an aspect of your life, but it's not a defining characteristic.

> Father, acknowledging my struggles is important, but defining myself by them can make it harder for me to experience the freedom You have for me. Help me with this. Amen.

IDENTITY SHIFT

The Holy Spirit was given to us as a promise that we will receive everything God has for us. God's Spirit will be with us until God finishes His work of making us complete. God does this to show His shining-greatness.
EPHESIANS 1:14

You *do* want to be defined by victory and by what God has promised.

While anxiety may be *something you battle*, it should not *define who you are*. What defines you is your victory in Christ. Even in the midst of ongoing, daily struggles with anxiety, you can have victory as you depend on God, His Word, and your Christian community.

Victory is yours every day that you seek God and continue pushing back against the effects of sin and brokenness on your life.

Let me tell you something extraordinary about who you are: *you are a child of God.* Can you even fathom the depth of that truth? It means that the good Creator of this amazing universe, the one who painted the skies with stars and breathed life into existence, claims *you* as His very own. *You are His.*

Being a child of God means that you have inherent worth and value. You are loved and cherished by the one who created you. And He has promised to give you victory.

> Father, help me to remember that my identity is in You and not in anything I battle. Amen.

THE JUGGLING ACT

He gives us everything we need for life and for holy living. He gives it through His great power. As we come to know Him better, we learn that He called us to share His own shining-greatness and perfect life.
2 PETER 1:3

You can do hard things. You *have* done hard things. But you can't do *everything*.

Let's consider each of those statements:

You can do hard things. God has given you everything you need to conquer the biggest challenges in your life. Second Peter tells us that God has given us everything we need for life and for holy living. No exceptions. Whatever challenges you face, you have what you need to overcome them.

You have done hard things. Already in your life, you've faced many challenges and overcome them. Your battle with anxiety is just one more hard thing God is going to give you the strength to overcome.

But you can't do everything. Throughout this book, we've talked about our limitations. It may feel sometimes like everything in your world demands your attention and energy. But let me remind you: you are a human being, not a superhero. You have limits given to you for your good by your good God.

> Father, when I feel discouraged or overwhelmed by my limitations, please remind me that You can do everything and that You are always with me. Amen.

OUT OF CONTROL

"Can you find out the deep things of God? Can you find out how far the All-powerful can go? They are higher than the heavens. What can you do? They are deeper than the place of the dead. What can you know? They are longer than the earth and wider than the sea."
JOB 11:7–9

Lean in and listen closely to this truth because understanding this truth now could change your future: *life is full of big things that are completely out of your control.*

Many of us would prefer to dictate every twist and turn, every outcome or circumstance. Feeling like we're in control gives us a sense of security and predictability. But *being controlling* is only a convincing forgery for *being in control*. We're still not actually in control of anything.

Here's the secret: the greatest growth in our lives often comes from surrendering our control to God and trusting Him no matter what. Yes, it can be uncomfortable. Yes, we may always wish we could have more influence over various aspects of our lives.

But by focusing on what we can influence and trusting God with what we can't, we are better able to release our anxiety and live to the fullest.

In the following devotions, let's look at five things you and I have no control over.

> Father, You are in control, and I am not. Help me to accept that and trust You completely. Amen.

WHAT IN THE WORLD?

God is our safe place and our strength. He is always our help when we are in trouble. So we will not be afraid, even if the earth is shaken and the mountains fall into the center of the sea.
Psalm 46:1–2

We have no control over *world events*.

Natural disasters, political conflicts, and global pandemics are completely out of our control. So if world news is too stressful for you, watch it in limited amounts. Or even take a break from it entirely. *Pay attention to what you pay attention to.*

I used to be a total news junkie, getting my news from multiple outlets and talking about world events with anyone who would listen. I also loved watching true crime shows and consumed them like candy. But then I noticed it was starting to affect my anxiety. I would lie awake at night and worry about things completely out of my control.

Bad news sells. Sensationalized stories get more attention. Negative news—especially involving conflicts, disasters, or tragedies—evokes strong emotional responses like fear or outrage, so media outlets love to lead with them. And strong emotional responses often feed anxiety.

If there's something you really need to know about, someone in your life will tell you.

> Father, when I'm tempted to worry about what's happening in the world, remind me to stop and pray instead of fear. Amen.

SOMETIMES YOU LOSE

*He heals those who have a broken
heart. He heals their sorrows.*
PSALM 147:3

We have no control over loss. I wish this weren't true.

Loss can take many forms—including loss of loved ones, relationships, health, possessions, or opportunities. Loss hurts because it involves separation from something or someone we love.

And it's okay that loss hurts. We can be confident that grieving a loss isn't sin, because when Jesus' friend Lazarus died, the Bible records that Jesus was "very sad and He was troubled" (John 11:33). Two verses later, He wept.

If anyone should be confident and joyful in the midst of loss, it would be Jesus; yet He demonstrated for us that grieving loss is the right and healthy response.

But Jesus never worried about loss, and neither should we. We certainly shouldn't worry about loss that may or may not even happen in the future. Often, the worries that lead to our anxiety involve losses that haven't happened yet.

A wise friend once told me, "You can either dread losing someone and suffer every time you imagine it, or you can enjoy the people and events in your life and be sad if you ever actually lose them."

> Father, please teach me to cherish and appreciate the time I have with people I love rather than allowing fear to consume me. Amen.

ON CHANGE

*"For I, the Lord, do not change. So you,
O children of Jacob, are not destroyed."*
MALACHI 3:6

We have no control over *change*.

Change is a constant part of life. *People change. Circumstances change. Relationships change.*

On one hand, this is good news. Hard seasons will pass and things won't always be difficult. Things that bother you today may not always bother you the same way. *That's good change.*

On the other hand, some change can be upsetting. Especially if we liked things the way they were. People we love die or divorce. Friends we thought we'd always have in our lives move on from us or move away. Dreams we carried for our future crumble like sand.

So when we're faced with uncomfortable seasons of change, we have two choices: *First, we can resist change.* We can dig our heels in and refuse to acknowledge or surrender to the new way of living. But this will always lead to increased frustration and discontentment.

Second, we can accept change. This mindset requires us to let go of "the way things should have been" and open our hearts and minds to new possibilities.

Father, thank You for giving me the confidence
in Malachi 3 that You never change.
You are dependable in every way. Amen.

TURNS OUT

"For My thoughts are not your thoughts, and My ways are not your ways," says the Lord. "For as the heavens are higher than the earth, so are My ways higher than your ways, and My thoughts than your thoughts."
ISAIAH 55:8–9

Something else we have no control over: *outcomes*.

Like the perfect ending in our favorite book or movie, we would love to control how things turn out in life, wouldn't we? But here's the truth we must learn to accept: we are not responsible for how things turn out—we are only responsible to *do right*.

In almost every situation, numerous details exist outside our control that can influence a final outcome. The attitudes and decisions of others, for example, play an important role in how a situation resolves.

Since we cannot control everything, here's what we do: We focus our energy and attention on *our* efforts, actions, and responses. We make the wisest choices possible, and we do our best in each situation. *And then we leave the outcome to God.*

This desire to control outcomes often comes from a fear of the unknown. But when we try to micromanage outcomes, we become hyperaware of every risk. And in trying to eliminate or manage every risk, we create anxiety.

> Father, You alone are in charge of outcomes, and so I trust You with them. Amen.

LOVE UNLEASHED

You obey the whole Law when you do this one thing, "Love your neighbor as you love yourself." But if you hurt and make it hard for each other, watch out or you may be destroyed by each other.
GALATIANS 5:14–15

We have no control over *other people*.

Specifically, we don't control their motives, opinions, or choices. And this is a very good thing. If we had control over other people, we wouldn't really have relationships with other people—we'd have relationships with other versions of ourselves.

Love, as taught in the Bible, is far more than a sentimental feeling we have for somebody else. It's an active commitment to seek that person's good. Biblical love is rooted in God's love for others—as ultimately demonstrated by Jesus' sacrifice of Himself on their behalf.

Instead of sacrificing the good of other people for our comfort, we should seek to sacrifice our comfort for the good of other people.

Our lack of control over other people is why we cannot search for our worth or approval from anyone other than God. Other people will let us down. It's human nature. This can look like rejection, criticism, or disapproval, which can send anxiety into high gear if we let it.

We shouldn't try to control other people, nor should we allow others to control us.

> Father, You are the only one with the right to control people. Help me to remember that. Amen.

LET IT GO

Christ was before all things. All things are held together by Him.
COLOSSIANS 1:17

Let's talk about why it's *good* that we're not actually in control.

On a surface level, being in control sounds amazing, doesn't it? If we were in control, things would always turn out the way we want. What would we have to worry about?

Answer: *everything*.

With control comes immense responsibility for outcomes. The weight of making the right decisions to ensure the welfare of everyone in our control would be an overwhelming burden we were not created to carry. We wouldn't even want to be in full control of ourselves if we understood everything involved.

If we were in control, the constant scrutiny, criticism, and blame for every choice we made would lead to immense pressure and a terrifying fear of failure. Our people-pleasing tendencies would be in constant war with what we believed would actually be best.

The constant decision-making and crisis management would eventually lead to burnout and decision fatigue. Our mistakes—especially the ones that hurt people we love—would be hard to forget or forgive. Without being all-knowing, all-powerful, and all-loving, being in control of ourselves and others would be a nightmare.

> Father, You are good at being God. Help me to remember that when I want control. Amen.

LOVE YOUR LIMITS

"O Lord, You have great power, shining-greatness and strength. Yes, everything in heaven and on earth belongs to You. You are the King, O Lord. And You are honored as head over all."
1 CHRONICLES 29:11

We are fearfully and wonderfully made, but we are not infinite.

We have boundaries—physical, spiritual, emotional—intended to protect us. We were never meant to be superheroes, always strong, always perfect.

Yet, within those limits, we have the extraordinary opportunity to encounter the limitless love and grace of God. In our limitations, we discover our need for someone greater than ourselves. We remember our dependence on the one who is infinite, the one who sustains all things.

In a world that often demands that we be more, achieve more, and do more, we must stubbornly acknowledge the limits imposed on us by our Creator. We have finite energy, resources, and abilities—just as we should. When we recognize our limits, we acknowledge God for who He is, and we accept ourselves for who we are.

John 1:3 tells us, "He made all things. Nothing was made without Him making it."

So in the following devotions, let's discuss five of our limitations that exist for our own good.

> Father, the world wants me to believe that I have unlimited agency and power, but I know that belongs to You. Help me to remember that limits are good. Amen.

TIME LIMITS

*Teach us to understand how many days we have.
Then we will have a heart of wisdom to give You.*
PSALM 90:12

We have limited *time*.

Specifically, we have limited days in our lifetime, and we have limited hours in our days.

As much as we may want to do it all, we can't do limitless things because we don't have limitless time. This is by God's design. In Psalm 139:16, David writes, "Your eyes saw me before I was put together. And all the days of my life were written in Your book before any of them came to be."

Have you ever wished our twenty-four-hour day could be longer?

Great idea, except we would fill those hours as well, and we would wish we had more.

We must learn to make good choices about how we spend our days—prioritizing certain activities over others based on their importance, urgency, and contribution to our goals and values.

Understanding and accepting that we can't do everything will be the work of our lifetime. Only God can do everything. Only God has limitless time and resources.

> Father, I acknowledge that time is a precious treasure. Help me learn to spend my time in ways that honor You. Amen.

BATTLE FATIGUE

"Come to Me, all of you who work and have heavy loads. I will give you rest."
MATTHEW 11:28

We have limited *energy*.

There's a fine line between doing our *best* and doing *it all*. Between being *kind* to everyone and being *everything* to everyone.

But when we push ourselves beyond the limits God placed for us, we deplete the energy reserves He has given us, and we sacrifice things that truly matter—things like rest.

When we feel constantly drained, exhausted, or overwhelmed, that's the sign that we need to stop and reevaluate the choices we're making. Acknowledging our limited energy is not weakness; it's wisdom.

Consider this: If God, who is infinitely powerful and capable, chose to rest on the seventh day in the creation week, what does that say about the importance of rest for us, His children? Among other important lessons, it reveals the wisdom and intentionality of our Creator.

Rest is not negotiable; it's Christlike.

When we honor our limited energy and rest in regular, healthy intervals, we actually have greater capacity to do our best at the things God has called us to do. It's easier to do right when we're not exhausted!

> Father, You are the good Creator, and in Your wisdom You established the healthy rhythm of work and rest. Help me honor Your plan and rest when I need to. Amen.

THE MULTITASKING TRAP

God is able to do much more than we ask or think through His power working in us. May we see His shining-greatness in the church. May all people in all time honor Christ Jesus. Let it be so.
EPHESIANS 3:20–21

We have limited *ability*.

It's hard to see limited ability as a good thing because our culture loves to celebrate limitless potential and extraordinary achievements. It's easy to overlook the value and lessons within our limitations.

But our limitations are *good* and *right* because they were given to us by God.

It was never God's design for any one person to be the best at everything. You have something specific God has designed for you to contribute to your friends, family, community, and church.

When we try too hard to be good at everything we do, we easily fall into the traps of high performance pressure, paralyzing fear of failure, and unhelpful social comparison.

And none of those traps help us excel at what God wants us to do. God will always equip us to accomplish the tasks He wants us to do. Our only job is to be faithful.

Father, thank You for the good gifts You have given me. Help me not to become distracted by the gifts or assignments You've given others. Amen.

ON BRAND

*My God will give you everything you need
because of His great riches in Christ Jesus.*
PHILIPPIANS 4:19

We have limited *resources*.

We live in a part of the world that equates success and worth with abundance and accumulation. *What do you own? What brands do you wear? How much money do you make?*

The pressure to accumulate more and more can become overwhelming. The fear of not having enough can consume us, leading to worry and stress. Styles change. Fads fade. Trends come and go in the blink of an eye.

The fear of missing out or being left behind by what we do or don't have can be profoundly distressing if we attach too much of our identity to *things*.

In Luke 12:15, Jesus was teaching His followers when He said, "Watch yourselves! Keep from wanting all kinds of things you should not have. A man's life is not made up of things, even if he has many riches."

So here are two things to remember: First, our worth is not determined by what we own. Second, God has been very generous to us. We have the ability to shift our focus away from what we *lack* to what we *have*.

Father, rich or poor, I'll never have enough if I fail to be content. Help me appreciate what You've provided. Amen.

A KIND COMMAND

Trust in the Lord with all your heart, and do not trust in your own understanding.
PROVERBS 3:5

We have limited *knowledge*.

Proverbs 3:5 is one of the most familiar verses in the Bible, yet it is one we struggle to take to heart. Why does God tell us not to trust our own understanding? Answer: because our knowledge is *limited* but His is *limitless*.

It is actually a kind thing for God to tell us to trust *Him* instead of ourselves. From the beginning of time, human beings have desired limitless knowledge and the ability to rest on our own wisdom. This sin got the first couple in trouble in the garden of Eden when they chose to eat from the tree of knowledge. And wanting limitless knowledge has been one of our great stumbling blocks ever since.

We have limited knowledge. The problem isn't actually that we want information. The problem is that we want to trust information instead of trusting God. If we're honest, many of us are more comfortable trusting facts than we are having faith. The only mysteries we enjoy are the ones in books—not the ones in real life.

> Father, the greatest knowledge I could ever have is found in the pages of my Bible where You have given me everything I need for life and godliness. Thank You. Amen.

FREED FROM CONTROL

"The God Who made the world and everything in it is the Lord of heaven and earth. He does not live in buildings made by hands. No one needs to care for Him as if He needed anything. He is the One Who gives life and breath and everything to everyone."
ACTS 17:24–25

As we've seen, limitations are a gift.

Limitations push us to rely on God. God wants us to acknowledge our dependence on Him for our physical and spiritual needs. If we had no limitations, we might be tempted to believe we didn't actually need God for anything.

Limitations encourage us to ask for help from others. We've seen throughout this book that we were made to exist in community. Even before sin entered the world, God said, "It is not good for man to be alone" (Genesis 2:18).

Asking for help from others creates a relationship where others can support and rely on us as well. This reciprocal relationship fosters a sense of community and encourages a culture of mutual respect and care.

Trying to live without the help of others is futile and foolish and not at all the way God designed our lives to be lived.

Father, please help me embrace my limitations as an invitation to lean on You and depend on the support and love of those around me. Amen.

NOT MAD, JUST DISAPPOINTED

*Do you think I am trying to get the favor of men,
or of God? If I were still trying to please men,
I would not be a servant owned by Christ.*
GALATIANS 1:10

So, what happens when we disappoint people because of our limitations?

Maybe you turn down an invitation to an opportunity because you've already committed your time to someone else. Or maybe you say no to something because you're trying to prioritize rest.

People may express their disappointment over your lack of participation. *What then?*

Saying no can be a challenging and uncomfortable experience, especially if you haven't done it very often. We naturally fear disappointing people because we care about their feelings and want to maintain good relationships.

But here's the truth we have to accept at some point: we cannot please everyone all the time. Saying no for the right reasons is not a sign of failure or inadequacy. It actually takes great courage to make decisions based on facts instead of feelings. The fact someone doesn't like your "no" doesn't mean you made the wrong choice.

Saying no when it's the right decision is far better than saying yes when it's the wrong decision.

> Father, please give me discernment to say yes and no at the right times. And then help me trust You regardless of how people respond. Amen.

HIDING AWAY

*Do not work only for your own good.
Think of what you can do for others.*
1 CORINTHIANS 10:24

Anxiety is an *isolator*.

Anxiety often looks like perfectionism in girls. But perfectionism and control actually drive us away from the life-giving relationships we're meant to enjoy with God and with others.

Anxiety is a master at building walls around our hearts and minds. Anxiety distorts our perception, convincing us—despite the overwhelming statistics that tell a different story—that our struggles are unique and nobody else could possibly understand our situation.

We may be tempted to isolate when we're struggling with anxiety because we have an overwhelming fear of being judged or negatively evaluated by others. This fear can cause us to be hesitant around others. We can become overly concerned with being misunderstood or criticized.

The answer: *think of what you can do for others.* By actively engaging in conversations, listening attentively, and showing genuine interest in others, we can actually redirect our thoughts and break down the unhelpful walls around our hearts and minds.

> Father, You know that evil wants to isolate us. So please help me fight the desire to hide when I'm struggling. Amen.

GIVE IT A REST

Show me Your ways, O Lord. Teach me Your paths. Lead me in Your truth and teach me. For You are the God Who saves me. I wait for You all day long.
PSALM 25:4–5

So, what *don't* you do when you can't fix something? Said another way: What *shouldn't* you do when faced with something that's impossible for you to handle?

First, don't *overreact to it*. Constantly reacting to external events with feelings of fear, anger, outrage, and isolation takes its toll on us over time. We weren't made to react to everything.

For thousands of years, people knew only what was happening in their community or village. This is the way we were designed to function in the world—to care about the tragedies of our families and community. Now with the twenty-four-hour news cycle and social media, we hear about every catastrophe and personal sadness. It's too much for the human heart to handle.

Second, don't *dwell on it*. Constantly thinking about something we can't fix can hold us hostage to heavy feelings and negative emotions. If you find yourself stuck thinking about something hard or impossible, talk to a parent or trusted mentor about it.

And then leave it in God's hands.

> Father, You're the one with the power to do something about all the sadness in the world. Help me trust You with it. Amen.

IN A FIX

Let me hear Your loving-kindness in the morning, for I trust in You. Teach me the way I should go for I lift up my soul to You.
PSALM 143:8

What do we do when we can't fix something? *We pray, surrender, and trust.*

First, we *pray*. Talking to God about the details of our lives is always the right decision. In situations where we can't fix something, prayer allows us to ask God for His direction and clarity.

Second, we *surrender*. Surrendering involves letting go of our attempts to control outcomes, desires, or expectations. When we surrender, we release our grip on a person or situation and acknowledge that we are not ultimately in charge.

Third, we *trust*. We choose to believe that God has a good, overarching plan for our lives, even if we can't see or understand a current outcome or situation. Trusting God allows us to release our need for control and accept that He has a purpose for every situation.

Note: Choosing to accept that we can't fix something isn't the same as passively resigning ourselves to something we don't like. Because of the way God wired you to care, you may always feel emotions about things you can't fix. But acceptance enables you to focus on what you *can* control.

> Father, help me to pray, surrender, and trust when I can't fix something. Amen.

BATTLE IN THE BIBLE

We break down every thought and proud thing that puts itself up against the wisdom of God. We take hold of every thought and make it obey Christ.
2 CORINTHIANS 10:5

God gave us His Word to help us fight anxiety and depression. Reading the Bible reminds us of God's character, promises, and faithfulness—all of which make praying, surrendering, and trusting the natural choices. Here are three things we find in the Bible when we're anxious:

- *We discover comfort.* The psalms, for example, are packed with comfort in God's presence. Reading the Bible stories reminds us that God's faithfulness extends throughout history.
- *We uncover truth.* Truth is necessary to renew our minds the way Romans 12:2 urges us. Often, God will graciously lead us to the exact passages and truths we need to fight whatever battle looms before us.
- *We receive renewal.* Specifically, Romans 12:2 teaches us to renew our minds. By reading and studying God's Word for ourselves, we learn to replace our anxious thoughts with the truth we see in scripture.

Father, Your Word enables me to anchor my thoughts to Your perspective, which brings peace beyond my understanding. Thank You. Amen.

NO SILVER BULLET

*Give your way over to the Lord.
Trust in Him also. And He will do it.*
PSALM 37:5

Willpower is not the answer to anxiety and depression.

Willpower, also known as self-control or self-discipline, is typically good. It's the ability to carefully control our thoughts, emotions, and behaviors to achieve specific goals or to resist temptations. It requires effort, focus, and perseverance—*all helpful things*.

But overcoming anxiety and depression usually requires more than simply gritting our teeth and summoning up a strong will to overcome.

So why is willpower not the silver bullet for anxiety and depression? *Willpower relies on self.*

Willpower only goes so far and works for so long. Willpower is a finite resource that becomes depleted over time. Like a muscle, our willpower eventually gets fatigued with too much use.

When we rely on our willpower to do big things, we often find ourselves running out of steam and unable to cross the finish line. *We were never meant to be the answer to our battle with anxiety and depression.*

It is hard to sustain our own efforts for the long run. We need something or someone who is infinitely stronger than we are. His name is Jesus.

> Father, I surrender my willpower to You, acknowledging that true and lasting transformation comes from surrendering my life to You. Amen.

LIVING HOPE

Hope never makes us ashamed because the love of God has come into our hearts through the Holy Spirit Who was given to us.
ROMANS 5:5

What is biblical hope? Here are four things to know: First, *biblical hope is not whimsical*. More than a feeling or emotion, it is an active and courageous choice—a deliberate decision to take God at His word. In the English language, we often use *hope* in a wishful way:

I hope we get a day off school.
I hope I got an A on that test.
I hope Mom makes spaghetti for supper.

But biblical hope is far more than wishful thinking. What has God promised? Do you believe it?

Second, *hope is a way of thinking*—it informs our goals, our choices, and our actions. We don't feel our way into hope; we think our way into it.

Third, *hope is learned*. It does not come naturally to human beings. We must choose to hope in God, even when life doesn't make sense.

Finally, *hope makes all the difference in our lives*. Reasoning with anxiety doesn't always make a difference since the world is full of things we can be anxious about. But hope? Real, durable hope in God will change us from the inside out.

> Father, I know that if my hope is tethered to Your unchanging promises, then peace will be the logical result. Help me hope in You. Amen.

HOPE SPRINGS ETERNAL

*"The Lord is my share," says my soul,
"so I have hope in Him."*
LAMENTATIONS 3:24

Hope is not the same as the power of positive thinking. Not even close.

Hope isn't the idea of plastering a smile on your face and thinking happy thoughts while the world around you burns to the ground. It isn't a magical solution that suddenly erases every challenge and hardship in your life. It's way deeper and far better than any of that.

Hope is a certainty in our souls that steadies us, even in the face of adversity. Hope acknowledges the reality of our circumstances and is rooted in the goodness and trustworthiness of God. We have hope that everything painful in our lives will work together for our good not because it's logical or probable, but because God promised it.

Hebrews 11:1 says, "Now faith is being sure we will get what we hope for. It is being sure of what we cannot see." "Being sure of what we cannot see" is the confident expectation we have that God is good and will keep His promises to us no matter what.

Hope is certainty, but hope is also a person. And that person has committed Himself to you. We'll talk more about that in the next devotion.

> Father, thank You for the assurance that I can hope and trust in You. Amen.

THE CASE FOR HOPE

Why are you sad, O my soul? Why have you become troubled within me? Hope in God, for I will yet praise Him, my help and my God.
PSALM 42:11

....

If we're going to hang on to hope, we'd better be sure of what our hope is in.

In a world that often disappoints us and leaves us longing for something more, our souls find their rest and security only in relying on the one who is steadfast and faithful.

Hope is an acknowledgment that we are not sufficient on our own and we are depending on a loving and trustworthy God. Hope is an invitation to surrender our exhausting striving and to place our confidence in the one who holds all things together in His hand.

Our hope, when placed in God, is not based on feeling or circumstances—good or bad—or our own abilities but on the unchanging character and promises of the one who sent His Son to die for us. Could there ever truly be anyone we could trust more than that?

Next, let's talk about four important things we need to know about hope.

> Father, like the psalmist said in Psalm 62, my soul is quiet and waits for You alone. My hope comes from You. Amen.

GREAT EXPECTATION

I would have been without hope if I had not believed that I would see the loving-kindness of the Lord in the land of the living. Wait for the Lord. Be strong. Let your heart be strong. Yes, wait for the Lord.
Psalm 27:13–14

Hope is *expectation*.

As we see so clearly in the Bible, hope is more than wishful thinking or vague optimism. It is rooted in the confident expectation that God will keep His promises and fulfill His purposes.

Hope is the joyful anticipation of what God has promised. It is not simply a vague longing but an active trust that enables us to get out of bed and do the next right thing, even on days when our hearts are heavy or our minds are conflicted.

Imagine learning you were going to inherit a billion dollars. You start living like you're rich. You take trips and buy clothes and give generously. You've banked on that money before you've ever seen it. That may not be the wisest way to respond to a potential inheritance because it relies on the promises of man.

But when it comes to relying on the promises God has made, you can go ahead and live like they're as good as fulfilled.

God always, always, *always* keeps His word.

> Father, thank You that Your promises are only and always true. Amen.

DO YOU REMEMBER?

This I remember, and so I have hope. It is because of the Lord's loving-kindness that we are not destroyed for His loving-pity never ends. It is new every morning. He is so very faithful.
LAMENTATIONS 3:21–23

Hope is *a way of thinking*.

Lamentations 3:21 begins with these words: "But this I remember." This action of *remembering* is linked to hope.

The discipline of *remembering* is intentionally recalling and reflecting on the teachings, truths, and works of God as revealed in the Bible. It is also intentionally recalling how God has been good and faithful to you in the past.

A mind that is controlled by biblical hope thinks beyond current circumstances—good or bad. It refuses to be held captive by negativity, fear, anxiety, or despair. It recognizes and believes that God is good and sovereign over every difficulty. It trusts in His unwavering care and clings to His steadfast promises, even in the face of grief or uncertainty.

A mind that is controlled by biblical hope is able to face trials with courage, knowing that God has no intent to harm but to bless.

> Father, please help me to remember Your faithfulness in the past so that I can better trust Your faithfulness in the present and future. Amen.

(NOT) EASY-PEASY LEMON SQUEEZY

*Be strong. Be strong in heart,
all you who hope in the Lord.*
PSALM 31:24

Hope *takes courage*.

Despite all the things I have written in these pages, I don't want to give you the impression that hope is easy or natural.

We live in a world that bombards us with negativity and cynicism. We face daily personal disappointments and global crises that can easily erode our hope—especially if you're wired to care deeply about the needs, experiences, and feelings of those around you.

Yet, all of God's commands in the Bible were written for us—including His command to *be courageous*.

Hope requires courage. It requires us to confront our fears and uncertainties. It demands that we face the very real possibility of disappointment. Yet, even in the face of these obstacles, hope requires that we persevere.

As you face moments of anxiety or depression, will you always choose the right response? Will you always take the next right step and say the right thing? Not if you're human (and I'm assuming you're human).

When you fail, it's not the end of your story. If you find yourself face down in the dirt, take a deep breath and find the courage to get back up and hope in God.

> Father, I know hope requires that I get back up and try again. Please give me courage. Amen.

HOLDING ON TO HOPE

*Let us hold on to the hope we say we have
and not be changed. We can trust God
that He will do what He promised.*
HEBREWS 10:23

Hope is *learned*.

The fact that we are encouraged to hold on to our hope means hope is something we can learn to do. Hope is a mindset and a perspective that should be nurtured over time. We are not born with hope—we learn it throughout our lifetime. Just as we learn to walk, to read, or to ride a bike, we can learn to hope.

The next time something hard or hurtful happens, stop and evaluate your response. Are you going to give in to the natural desire to sink into the pit of despair, or are you going to have the courage to hope? Are you going to believe all is lost and nothing will ever be right in your world again, or will you choose to believe that God is good and sovereign and able to bring good from your painful circumstances?

Learning hope requires us to slow down and evaluate. It requires us to say the right things to ourselves even before we feel them. It requires us to meditate on truth instead of meditating on our fears.

Father, most of the time it would be easier to worry than to hope, but worry doesn't bring You glory. So help me learn to hope in You. Amen.

SHARING IS CARING

Let us thank the God and Father of our Lord Jesus Christ. It was through His loving-kindness that we were born again to a new life and have a hope that never dies. This hope is ours because Jesus was raised from the dead.
1 PETER 1:3

One important, often-overlooked reason for our hope: *ours is a living hope.*

There's a lot of chaos in the world today, but we can have hope because the one who secured it for us is alive.

As we've seen in previous pages, our hope is rooted in something far more enduring than anything this tired, broken world can offer. Our hope finds its source in the person and work of Jesus Christ. In Him we have assurance of salvation, the promise of eternal life, and the hope of being reconciled to God.

As this living hope takes root in our hearts and minds, it begins to shape our perspective of people around us. It compels us to participate in God's redemptive work—to be agents of hope and healing in a hurting world.

When this living hope changes our lives, we can't help but tell others about it.

Father, please give me opportunities to share with others the incredible hope You've given me. Amen.

THE LONELINESS EPIDEMIC

Turn to me and show me Your loving-kindness. For I am alone and in trouble.
PSALM 25:16

One factor that contributes to anxiety: a loneliness epidemic.

There are many culprits, but here are two:

First, *we're spending too little time with people.* Ongoing cultural trends have resulted in less connection to family, neighbors, and local communities, leading to increased loneliness and isolation. We are often taught to value individuality over community.

When was the last time you prioritized spending quality time with a friend or family member? When was the last time you were fully present and attentive, putting away distractions and actively listening and engaging in meaningful conversation?

Second, *we're spending too much time with technology.* I'm truly not trying to be the technology police in this book—I see the benefits of technology. But just as it has enabled us to stay connected in many ways, it has also led to a shift in the quality and depth of our relationships.

Virtual interactions, social media platforms, and digital communication cannot replace face-to-face, in-person relationships. They just can't. An abundance of research continues to support this reality. Yet, culturally, we're spending more time on devices than we are with people we love, which is leading us to feel isolated and alone.

> Father, especially when I am lonely, give me the courage and wisdom to step away from technology and sit down with people I love. Amen.

TAKE THIS PROMISE TO THE BANK

*The Lord is near to all who call on Him,
to all who call on Him in truth.*
PSALM 145:18

God is always near. There isn't a moment you call on Him that He is not willing or able to respond to you. He wants you to talk to Him.

The presence of God is a comforting and constant reality for those who believe in Him. Scripture is filled with promises and assurances of God's nearness to His people:

Psalm 34:18: "The Lord is near to those who have a broken heart. And He saves those who are broken in spirit."

Psalm 46:1: "God is our safe place and our strength. He is always our help when we are in trouble."

God is not a distant or detached deity. He is a loving, ever-present Father who desires to be part of our lives. He wants to help you with whatever you feel or face.

So how much time do you spend with God? How's your attitude toward Him?

> Father, thank You for walking with me every moment. You are truly my refuge and strength, my ever-present help in times of trouble. Help me learn to turn to You first. Amen.

THE SECRET SAUCE

He answered me, "I am all you need. I give you My loving-favor. My power works best in weak people." I am happy to be weak and have troubles so I can have Christ's power in me.
2 CORINTHIANS 12:9

One of the reasons we struggle to be with people is we struggle with vulnerability.

The word *vulnerable* comes from the Latin word *vulnerare*, which means "to wound" or "to injure."

Vulnerability in relationships requires us to shed our armor—to strip away the unnecessary layers of protection we've built around our hearts—in order to be real and honest with people. Vulnerability is what enables us to have conversations that go deeper than surface level.

What are your struggles?
What is God teaching you?
What are your dreams and hopes for your future?

Let me be honest with you: in having conversations like these, we open ourselves up to the possibility of rejection, disappointment, and pain. People may misuse the things we share. They may not be vulnerable in response to our vulnerability.

Yes, when we are vulnerable, we are woundable. And yet vulnerability is the secret sauce that adds depth and richness to our relationships. If you want to get close to people, vulnerability is a risk you will need to take.

Somebody has to go first. Why not you?

> Father, I don't want to build walls around my heart. Please help me be vulnerable with others. Amen.

BEST RELATIONAL PRACTICES

*Try to understand other people. Forgive each other.
If you have something against someone, forgive
him. That is the way the Lord forgave you.*
COLOSSIANS 3:13

Let's talk about two of the best relational practices for teen girls: *be quick to apologize and quick to forgive.*

First, be quick to apologize for hurts you cause. Females often have a tendency to apologize excessively. For example, we apologize for scooting past someone in the grocery store. We apologize if our grocery cart touches someone else's cart. This is not what I'm talking about here. The Bible teaches that we should be quick to apologize when we know we've sinned against someone.

Even if the hurt was unintentional, we should be quick to make things right when we learn that someone was harmed by our words or choices.

Second, be quick to forgive when asked. When someone comes to us with a sincere apology, we have the unique opportunity to do what Jesus has done for us—to practice compassion and let go of the wrong done against us. We can even choose to forgive before the wrongs are righted or the hurt feelings are healed.

Life is full of these daily, tiny opportunities to practice courage and forgiveness.

> Father, help me to be quick to apologize and quick to forgive. I know this is evidence of someone who loves You and wants to be right with others. Amen.

CONTACT SPORT

Do not leave your own friend or your father's friend alone, and do not go to your brother's house in the day of your trouble. A neighbor who is near is better than a brother who is far away.
PROVERBS 27:10

Let's talk about the difference between *contact* and *connection*. On the surface, they look similar—but they are actually very different.

Contact is coming in touch with someone or communication with someone. It usually involves surface-level interactions—often brief or transactional in nature. This interaction can be a quick hug in the school hallway or a text message or comment on social media. It's typically a brief encounter.

Connection, on the other hand, goes much deeper than contact. It involves shared experience. It happens when two or more people share mutual understanding, trust, and time. It is meaningful and authentic. Connection requires active listening and a willingness to be present in each other's lives.

Contact is fleeting; connection endures.

Contact is not a bad thing. It is typically the spark that can lead to connection. But belonging and acceptance require connection. If you're lonely, look around. Is there someone in your life with whom you can connect?

Father, please give me the courage to step outside my comfort zone and build connections. Give me the words to say and the willingness to share from my own life. Amen.

JUST GO

*Let us not stay away from church meetings.
Some people are doing this all the time. Comfort each
other as you see the day of His return coming near.*
HEBREWS 10:25

Be with people more. Specifically, *go to church*. Be involved. Make it yours.

Going to church may seem cliché or like something the adults in your life nag you about, but there is something unique and important waiting for you within your local church walls. Church isn't just for adults. It's for you too. It's a place where you can find belonging, where you can worship in community, and where you can pursue a deeper relationship with God.

You need the church, and the church needs you.

Joining a good local church allows you to connect with like-minded teens and families who share your beliefs. It can also foster an important sense of belonging and provide you with a church family who can offer encouragement, friendship, accountability, and help during hard times.

How do you make church yours? Go faithfully. Take an active role in your community. Start conversations with anyone and everyone. Learn from others.

Yes, even if you are nervous at first.

> Father, I know good gifts are waiting for me
> in my local church if I just look for them.
> Help me to go and be faithful. Amen.

BUILDING MUSCLE

I have trusted in Your loving-kindness. My heart will be full of joy because You will save me. I will sing to the Lord, because He has been good to me.
PSALM 13:5–6

Building the muscle of trust takes work. But don't give up.

Unfortunately, we can't develop trust in isolation. It is always built and strengthened in the context of relationships—with friends, family, and God.

It starts by being honest and open with people in your life. It requires taking risks and facing potential disappointments. Yes, there will be times when people you trust let you down. It happens. You'll share something personal, and your friend will respond insensitively. Something that matters deeply to you won't be well received by someone else.

There will also be situations where *you* don't provide the response to your friend that she needs in that moment. It's part of being human.

In moments of relational stress or disappointment, you'll be tempted to throw in the towel, to choose isolation *because at least isolation doesn't say hurtful things*. But don't give up. Good things can come from relationships, even after hurts have happened. In fact, the healthiest relationships are ones in which people have been hurt, have forgiven, and have agreed to keep being friends.

> Father, please help me try (and try again!) to build good friendships, even when it gets discouraging. You understand rejection. Amen.

VIRTUAL REALITY

*Make the best use of your time.
These are sinful days. Do not be foolish.
Understand what the Lord wants you to do.*
EPHESIANS 5:16–17

Let's talk some more about technology. I know, *groan*.

I know much of your life relies on it—whether or not that's your choice.

But a book about anxiety and depression wouldn't be doing its job without talking about the scientific links between these battles and technology.

Instead of leading to increased relationships, smartphones are actually linked to increased loneliness, depression, and individualism. They are responsible for information overload, social media comparison, sleep disruption, and technostress (the pressure to respond to every message right away). By now you know technology blurs the boundaries between online life and real life.

Specifically, research says that teens who spend five to seven hours per day on their phones are twice as likely to become depressed.

Be mindful of your technology usage. Set boundaries with the help of a parent or trusted mentor. Practice good digital habits. Take regular breaks from your screens.

> Father, please give me wisdom to navigate the complexities of this digital age. I recognize the privileges and the pitfalls it contains. Amen.

SCREENS AND TEENS

Let me say it again. Have nothing to do with foolish talk and those who want to argue. It can only lead to trouble.
2 TIMOTHY 2:23

Let's talk briefly about some good technology practices for teen girls. Especially when fighting anxiety and depression, it's important to do these things:

- *Balance your screen time daily.* Set limits to ensure you have time for important face-to-face interactions, exercise, hobbies, and time with God.
- *Use your social media cautiously.* Ruthlessly avoid comparison, negativity, and mindless scrolling.
- *Guard your personal information carefully.* Never share sensitive details with strangers or on public platforms. Review the privacy settings of your social media to ensure they are set appropriately. Be suspicious of requests. When in doubt, ask a trusted adult.
- *Disconnect your technology regularly.* Give yourself breaks to recharge. Engage in activities that don't involve screens—such as reading or spending time outdoors. Not only does disconnection help reduce stress and improve focus, but it gives us the distance we need to better understand online interactions we've had.

If you ever get into a situation where you realize you've made a mistake or shared information that should have been kept private, get help from your parent or trusted mentor right away.

Father, You see and know all things. Help me practice good technology habits that please You. Amen.

CYBERBULLYING

You should be wise in what you say. Then the one who is against you will be ashamed and will not be able to say anything bad about you.
TITUS 2:8

As long as we're talking about technology, we need to discuss one more important thing: *cyberbullying.*

Cyberbullying uses technology to bully other people.

Let's state clearly that cyberbullying is never okay. It's hurtful, destructive, and has real-life consequences for teens who experience it. The command in Ephesians 4:32 to be kind to one another extends to the internet too. If you wouldn't say or accept the behavior face-to-face, you shouldn't say or accept the behavior online, either.

Two pieces of advice: *First, if you witness cyberbullying, don't be a silent bystander.* It's always the right thing to stand for what pleases God. Go to a parent or trusted authority and say what you've seen. If you can bring evidence, even better. Take a screenshot if possible.

Second, if someone is bullying you online—through means such as texts or private messages—tell your parent or a trusted adult. Don't keep these painful situations stuck inside your heart or mind. The person who has been unkind needs help, and you don't need to suffer silently.

> Father, please guard my heart and mind from all negative influences in the digital world, and give me the courage to say something if I see wrongdoing. Amen.

TRIGGERS FOR TRUST

He will not be afraid of bad news. His heart is strong because he trusts in the Lord.
PSALM 112:7

Let's talk about *triggers*.

The word *triggered* is a necessary word for people who have experienced trauma, but unfortunately, it has become a joke to many people because it has been overly used. Specifically, it has become a way to insult people who are perceived as too sensitive.

Nevertheless, here are two things you should know about triggers.

First, triggers are real, and they have real impact. Triggers are simply situations or words that evoke strong emotional responses based on previous experiences. Maybe the smell of a perfume reminds you of somebody you lost, or maybe seeing a happy family reminds you of what life used to be like before your parents divorced. Every day, life is full of reminders—both good and bad. We can't avoid them, nor can we allow them to dictate our moods or responses.

Second, we can learn to turn anxieties into triggers for trust. Even just learning to pray—*God, this is hard, but I trust You with this*—is a powerful prayer in a moment of sadness or uncertainty. And God always welcomes our cries for His help.

So let's talk about four common triggers for anxiety and depression.

> Father, this is hard, but I trust You. Amen.

CRITICAL LISTENING SKILLS

He whose ear listens to careful words spoken will live among the wise.
PROVERBS 15:31

Let's talk about *criticism*. Nobody loves it—everybody hears it. So, what do we do with it?

First, *stay calm*. Take a deep breath and avoid reacting impulsively or defensively. Being calm will enable you to think more clearly and respond more maturely. Refuse to be offended or take things personally, as doing so will get in the way of good communication.

Second, *listen actively*. Pay attention to what the person is saying. Avoid interrupting or dismissing their words. Truly consider what is being said.

Third, *evaluate carefully*. The words may be hard to hear, but is there any truth to what is being said? Are there areas where you could improve?

Fourth, *respond gracefully*. Choose your words and tone with utmost care. Be respectful—even if the person criticizing you wasn't kind. Genuinely express your gratitude for the feedback. If something was misunderstood, calmly and kindly provide an explanation.

It's absolutely normal to feel hurt or upset when faced with criticism, but Proverbs tells us that if we accept it, consider it, and apply necessary changes to our lives, we will live among the wise.

Father, I know how I respond to criticism says more about me than anything I could be criticized for. So help me respond in a way that honors You. Amen.

WHAT TO DO WITH REJECTION

*"If the world hates you, you know it
hated Me before it hated you."*
JOHN 15:18

Let's talk about *rejection*.

Jesus understands rejection. He spent His entire life serving others, and then He died for people who continue to reject Him every day. He faced rejection from religious leaders, political authorities, and even some of His closest friends and followers.

On the night before He would be crucified, Jesus faced personal betrayal from one of His closest disciples, Judas Iscariot, who betrayed Him to authorities for thirty pieces of silver.

Jesus understands rejection.

So here are some things to consider if you experience it: First, if somebody rejects you, it probably has less to do with you than it does to do with that person. People's opinions are typically influenced by many factors outside your control. So don't be quick to internalize the rejection or believe it is a reflection of your worth or value.

Second, instead of chasing after someone who hasn't demonstrated an interest in being your friend, spend the bulk of your time and energy with those who want to be your friend. Specifically, surround yourself with people who love Jesus and love you.

Father, despite being rejected, Jesus remained steadfast in His mission, demonstrating unwavering love and forgiveness to those around Him. Help me follow His good example. Amen.

TACKLING DOUBT

*Our life is lived by faith. We do not live
by what we see in front of us.*
2 CORINTHIANS 5:7

Let's talk about *doubt*.

Doubt is a natural part of life. Often we experience doubt about the things or people that are actually the most important to us. If we don't care about something or someone, why would we worry about them?

Specifically, when it comes to our faith, doubt can indicate we're engaging with our beliefs on a deeper level—wrestling with ideas to make sure we understand them.

When we grapple with doubt, we get to examine our beliefs, challenge our assumptions, and refine our understanding. It is through this process that we make our faith our own rather than simply accepting what someone else has told us.

What we do with our doubts is far more important than whether we have them. My advice: Surround yourself with people who love Jesus and are willing to listen and engage in thoughtful conversation. Don't seek out angry, bitter people who are primarily going to try and convert you to their anger or bitterness.

Look for people who will listen carefully and then point you to truth.

> Father, Your truth never changes, even when I'm struggling to understand or apply it. Give me wisdom to seek after Your truth at all times and in all situations. Amen.

ASLAN'S FACE

He has taken our sins from us as far as the east is from the west. The Lord has loving-pity on those who fear Him, as a father has loving-pity on his children. For He knows what we are made of. He remembers that we are dust.
PSALM 103:12–14

Let's talk about *guilt*.

Guilt is the deep feeling of shame or sadness that arises out of remorse or regret for things we have said or done in the past. Guilt can trigger anxiety.

In chapter 13 of *The Lion, the Witch, and the Wardrobe*, the White Witch reads Edmund's sins aloud for all to hear. Namely, she rightly accuses him of being a traitor. My favorite line in this chapter—and one of my favorite lines in the entire book—happens here. Even as the White Witch accused Edmund of his wrong choices, "Edmund was on the other side of Aslan, looking all the time at Aslan's face."

There is no way to escape guilt in this life. Romans 3:23 tells us that we all fall short of perfection. We all sin. And that sin results in guilt.

As you probably know, Aslan represents Jesus in *The Lion, the Witch, and the Wardrobe*, and C.S. Lewis taught us what we should do when we're rightly wracked by our own guilt: we should look to Jesus.

> Father, please help me turn toward You and not away when I feel guilt. Amen.

GRACE NOTES

Let us go with complete trust to the throne of God. We will receive His loving-kindness and have His loving-favor to help us whenever we need it.
HEBREWS 4:16

God has grace for you for *today*.

When we're experiencing anxiety, we're either stuck in the past or dwelling in the future.

Being stuck in the past looks like dwelling on past events, mistakes, or regrets. Maybe we replay negative memories like a movie reel in our heads, rehashing unhelpful things we've said, done, or experienced. This rumination can make our feelings of anxiety worse as our bodies and brains struggle to differentiate old memories from current reality.

Dwelling in the future looks like excessive worry about something that hasn't happened yet and may not happen at all. Maybe we're obsessed with what could go horribly wrong. This anticipation of grief or pain can act as gasoline on the fire of our anxiety.

Practical tip: Whenever you notice yourself starting to sit in the past or dwell in the future, imagine your thoughts as a movie and simply press PAUSE. Talk to God about whatever concerns you have and leave the rest to Him.

> Father, Your grace doesn't exist for me in the past or the future; it exists for me today. Help me be present and trust You with everything that is not today. Amen.

EXIT STRATEGIES

When my worry is great within me,
Your comfort brings joy to my soul.
PSALM 94:19

Anxiety is uncomfortable.

The rapid heartbeat, the shortness of breath, the tense muscles, the knotted stomach, the sweaty palms—most of us would do almost anything to escape anxiety's grip.

So, we often go to great lengths to numb or ease the discomfort—even if the choices we make to do it aren't helpful or healthy. Examples:

We may seek excessive reassurance from others. Asking and re-asking (and asking again!) for someone to reassure us about our decisions or talk us out of our fears may bring temporary relief. But this type of behavior can create new or additional problems, and it can actually perpetuate the cycle of anxiety.

We may overcommit. Staying busy so we don't have time to consider our anxiety can actually increase our stress levels and lead to burnout, which can perpetuate the cycle of anxiety. (Notice a trend?)

Two of the most common strategies for dealing with anxiety are escape and avoidance. We'll look closely at each of those in the next two devotions.

In the meantime, know this: our only true and lasting comfort when facing anxiety comes from God. So talk to Him, read His Word, and trust.

> Father, please help me learn healthy coping skills and strategies to combat my anxious thoughts and feelings. Thank You for always being near. Amen.

ESCAPE ROOM

*The Lord is near to those who have a broken heart.
And He saves those who are broken in spirit.*
PSALM 34:18

Let's talk specifically about *escape*.

While it's completely natural to seek ways to escape or avoid anxiety, certain behaviors can be unhelpful or even hurtful in the long run.

Let's look at a few examples of unhelpful escape strategies.

First, excessive screen time is an unhelpful escape strategy. Spending excessive amounts of time on screens—phones, computers, gaming consoles—can become a harmful way to avoid anxiety. Occasional usage is normal, but excessive usage to avoid difficult feelings is unhelpful.

Second, withdrawing from people is an unhelpful escape strategy. Avoiding social activities, shirking personal responsibilities, or isolating from family and friends may feel comforting at first, but loneliness can lead to increased anxiety symptoms and create further harm in the long run.

Third, overeating or undereating is an unhelpful escape strategy. Using any substance—food, drugs, alcohol—to avoid anxiety is deeply harmful and can negatively impact your health in the long run.

In moments of sadness, remember this: God has promised to be near you. You are never alone.

Father, I don't need unhealthy coping skills; I only need what You have already provided for me. You promise to meet all my needs. Thank You. Amen.

THE ART OF AVOIDANCE

My body and my heart may grow weak, but God is the strength of my heart and all I need forever.
PSALM 73:26

Avoidance is one common way to deal with situations or activities that trigger anxiety. We're faced with an uncomfortable situation and instead of facing it head-on, we avoid it by doing something that will distract us.

Let's look at some common examples of avoidance.

- *Procrastination.* Putting off tasks or responsibilities can temporarily relieve our discomfort, but sometimes this coping mechanism leads to last-minute pressures or increased stress that ends up intensifying our original anxiety symptoms.

- *Escapism.* Engaging in excessive screen time, video gaming, movie watching, or Netflix bingeing can offer us temporary relief, but it limits our ability to address the underlying issues of what is actually causing our anxiety. The cause for the anxiety doesn't actually go away—it just waits for us to finish our movie.

- *Risky behavior.* Self-harm, disordered eating, and unhealthy dating or relationships may temporarily alleviate anxiety because we're distracted, but these behaviors are harmful and can lead to serious physical and emotional consequences in addition to the anxiety that still exists underneath the behavior.

> Father, avoidance may provide relief in the moment, but it can actually reinforce my anxious thoughts. Please help me identify when I am avoiding. Amen.

AN EXPERIMENT WITH RISK

Even if an army gathers against me, my heart will not be afraid. Even if war rises against me, I will be sure of You.
PSALM 27:3

The answer to both escapism and avoidance: take risks and be brave.

When we have the courage to take risks and be brave in life, we discover talents, strengths, opportunities, and capabilities we never knew we had.

We meet people and experience things we never dreamed possible.

We learn things about ourselves and others we never would have learned about otherwise.

Does this mean it is easy to take risks and be brave? Not necessarily.

Life is filled with many wonderful opportunities, but they often require us to step outside our comfort zone and take a careful, calculated risk. This doesn't mean we put ourselves in danger or do things that are potentially harmful. But—listening to the wise counsel of the trusted people in our lives—we see an opportunity to start a new venture, to pursue a passion, or to embark on a fun adventure, *and we take it.*

> Father, please help me take risks and be brave. Help me trust that You have people for me to meet and lessons for me to learn outside my comfort zone. Amen.

WRITE THIS DOWN

Give teaching to a wise man and he will be even wiser. Teach a man who is right and good, and he will grow in learning.
PROVERBS 9:9

Have you ever wanted to try something new, but you were afraid of all the things that could go wrong? Taking risks and doing new things can be hard.

Examples: participating in music at your church, starting a new conversation with someone you don't know, taking a church trip, starting a new job, going to a new school, beginning a new habit. *The list is endless.*

If you get nervous when trying something new, you're not alone. In these moments of uncertainty, it's natural for doubts and fears to creep in. But instead of allowing our doubts and fears to win, what if we shifted our perspective slightly? That is, in every new, hard thing, we learned to say to ourselves, "It will either work out or it will become something I can learn from." Both of these possible outcomes offer us valuable lessons and opportunities for growth. They also change the goal from *being successful* to *doing our best.* And achieving this goal becomes possible no matter the outcome.

> Father, life is full of good things I'll miss if I'm too afraid to take healthy risks. So help me trust that it will either work out or be something I can learn from. Amen.

BREAKING FREE

Christian brother, you were chosen to be free. Be careful that you do not please your old selves by sinning because you are free. Live this free life by loving and helping others.
GALATIANS 5:13

As I said in an earlier devotion, anxiety and depression are liars. One of the lies they want you to believe is that you are powerless—that you'll be stuck in your anxiety and depression forever and there's nothing you can do about it.

But this simply isn't true.

Believing you're powerless to fight anxiety and depression is dangerous for many reasons. For example, it makes it easy to believe you're a victim rather than an active participant in fighting your anxiety. It limits your willingness to take risks and try new things—both of which are helpful when fighting anxiety. It leads you to believe your choices and actions make no difference, which can lead to feeling sad or hopeless about your situation.

In reality, you have agency over many things. And God is absolutely committed to helping you grow. In the words of Philippians 2:13, "He is working in you. God is helping you obey Him. God is doing what He wants done in you."

Over the next several devotions, let's look at our agency over five important areas of our lives.

> Father, help me refuse the lie that I have no agency in my battle with anxiety. Amen.

A LIKELY RESPONSE

God is the One Who gives us power over sin through Jesus Christ our Lord. We give thanks to Him for this.
1 CORINTHIANS 15:57

We have agency over our *responses*.

Regardless of the many things over which we do not have control, we do have agency when it comes to the way we respond to people and events. Three quick thoughts:

First, it's always a wise idea to pause before you respond. Don't allow your initial thoughts to be your response until you've given them careful consideration. Our gut reactions aren't always best or right.

Second, it's always a good idea to consider the consequences of your response before you say or do anything. You may want to vent, argue, or retaliate, but what could be the consequences of those decisions?

Finally, it's always the right decision to align your response with God's Word and His expectations of you. He's not aloof, detached, or disinterested in the way you respond. Remember, James 1:19 tells us to listen much, speak little, and be slow to become angry.

So, in the next few pages, let's talk about three responses to anxiety that we need to avoid: delaying, denying, and distracting.

> Father, please help my responses always to be a reflection of Your love, wisdom, and grace in my life. And when that doesn't happen, help me make it right. Amen.

JUST DO IT

*If you know what is right to do but
you do not do it, you sin.*
JAMES 4:17

One response we need to avoid: *delay*.

If you know you have something hard you need to do—a difficult conversation, a challenging homework assignment, a tiresome chore—don't put it off. Delay can feed anxiety and make everything worse.

We may think we're avoiding discomfort by putting off the difficult task or situation, but in reality we're spending energy worrying about it, anticipating it, and dreading it.

The answer: just do the thing that needs to be done. It may be uncomfortable, but you won't be any more comfortable being anxious about it.

Often, when we delay a conversation or situation, our what-if scenarios or low-grade dread is actually worse than the event itself. We don't usually assume the situation will go well, do we? Often our minds fill in the unknowns with worst-case scenarios. And by the time we do the difficult thing, it's worse than it would have been if we had just done it to begin with.

As James 4:17 tells us, "If you know what is right to do but you do not do it, you sin."

> Father, please help me just to do the thing that needs to be done. Delay is no better than the anxiety of dreading it. Amen.

LIVING IN DENIAL

*He who walks without blame and does what is right
and good, and speaks the truth in his heart.
He does not hurt others with his tongue, or do wrong
to his neighbor, or bring shame to his friend.*
PSALM 15:2–3

Another response we need to avoid: *denial*.

Denial can be a defense mechanism that temporarily shields us from facing the root cause of whatever is making us anxious.

We may be in denial because we want to avoid negative outcomes or consequences of whatever is making us uncomfortable. Denial affords us the opportunity to momentarily alleviate our anxiety by pretending the situation doesn't exist.

We may be in denial because we're scared of confronting the truth. Denial can temporarily protect us from fear and discomfort.

But it's important to understand that denial never works in the long run. And, in fact, it can make our anxiety worse over time. The false sense of control eventually intensifies the anxious feelings we're already suppressing.

In the words of Psalm 15:2, speak the truth to your heart, and then ask God to help you speak the truth to others.

> Father, help me acknowledge whatever truth
> needs to be acknowledged. Help me want to
> please You more than I want the comfort
> of postponing what is difficult. Amen.

FIX YOUR GAZE

Let your eyes look straight in front of you, and keep looking at what is in front of you. Watch the path of your feet, and all your ways will be sure.
PROVERBS 4:25–26

Another response we need to avoid: *distraction*.

Distraction is the coping mechanism that uses various activities to divert our attention away from whatever actually needs our attention in that moment.

Here are a few common distractions we turn to:

- *Social media.* We've already looked at our feeds. We've already interacted with our friends. And now what? We scroll. . .and scroll. . .and *scroll.*
- *Music.* Is there anything wrong with listening to music? Of course not. But listening to escape or to shift our focus away from something that needs our attention is actually a form of distraction. And that can be unhelpful.
- *Books and magazines.* Diving into a captivating series of novels or endlessly flipping through magazines can help transport our minds away from distressing or uncomfortable feelings.

The list of possible distractions is endless, but so are the consequences if we choose to distract instead of address whatever is causing our anxiety.

> Father, it's tempting to use distraction to fend off distressing or uncomfortable thoughts, feelings, or situations, but distraction offers only temporary relief. Help me trust You enough to handle whatever is troubling. Amen.

EXPECTATION MANAGEMENT

My soul is quiet and waits for God alone. He is the One Who saves me. He alone is my rock and the One Who saves me. He is my strong place. I will not be shaken.
Psalm 62:1–2

So, we have agency over our responses, but we also have agency over our *expectations*.

Expectations are the beliefs, assumptions, or anticipations we hold regarding how people, situations, or events should unfold or meet our firmly held criteria.

Having healthy expectations is motivating. In fact, research continues to show a direct link between happiness and reasonable expectations. But having unrealistic or unreasonable expectations for ourselves or others often leads to disappointment, frustration, or anxiety.

Having unrealistic expectations for others may look like being unnecessarily upset when our friends make mistakes, demanding constant availability from people, or imposing our goals and ambitions on those we love.

Setting unhelpful expectations for ourselves often happens when we compare our experiences or progress to someone else's and want the life she has instead of the life we've been given.

Here are three ways we can set healthy expectations: cultivate gratitude, celebrate growth, recognize progress.

> Father, please give me the wisdom to set and adjust my expectations when necessary and the ability to adapt when things don't go as planned. Amen.

DO IT WITH JOY

A glad heart is good medicine, but a broken spirit dries up the bones.
PROVERBS 17:22

We have agency over our responses and our expectations. We also have agency over our *joy*.

Sorrow is inevitable in this lifetime, but joy is not. Joy is accepted or refused. It isn't just something we *feel*; it's something we *choose*.

Having agency over our joy means we recognize and accept our ability to cultivate joy even during challenging circumstances.

Having agency over our joy means external circumstances and other people aren't responsible for our joy—*we are*. While recognizing that ultimate joy comes from God and is given by God's grace, we have the choice to respond to life's circumstances and actively pursue or deny joy.

Having agency over our joy means we actively engage in cultivating a joyful perspective by choosing to fix our minds on truth. Joy is largely a matter of where we put our attention. Will you focus on the things going wrong or the things going right?

By choosing to dwell on the promises of God found in the Bible, we allow joy to take root and grow in our hearts. Joy, therefore, is a type of resistance against despair.

> Father, joy is one of Your precious gifts to me. Please fill my heart with Your joy as I trust in You. Amen.

A CHOICE WORTH MAKING

"Good will come to the man who trusts in the Lord, and whose hope is in the Lord."
JEREMIAH 17:7

We have agency over our responses, our expectations, and our joy. We also have agency over our *hope*.

Hope comes from God, but we have the ability and responsibility to actively shape and cultivate our outlook and attitude in life.

What is biblical hope? It is. . .

- *Grounded in God's character.* Biblical hope is anchored in the reality that God is trustworthy, unchanging, and sovereign over all of life.
- *Rooted in God's promises.* Biblical hope believes God's promises to provide, protect, guide, save, and redeem. God's holiness depends on keeping His promises.
- *Focused on eternity.* Biblical hope acknowledges the reality of pain and suffering, but it looks beyond it to the hope of eternal life promised by God. This painful life is not all there is.
- *Centered on Christ.* Jesus only and always is the anchor for our hope. Biblical hope is inseparable from our relationship with Him. Because Jesus died and rose again, we have hope!
- *Impactful on our lives right now.* If our hope doesn't change our lives right now, it isn't biblical hope. Biblical hope doesn't just exist for eternity; it exists for us today.

> Father, I know hope is not a passive emotion but a deliberate choice. Help me hope in You. Amen.

RELEARNING REST

I will lie down and sleep in peace.
O Lord, You alone keep me safe.
PSALM 4:8

We also have agency over our *rest*.

Having agency over our rest means we recognize the importance of rest and consciously prioritize it even (and especially!) amid a demanding and busy life.

You may be thinking, *But I've got homework!* or *I don't choose my bedtime!* or *I can't fall asleep when I do go to bed!*

And it's true—many things stand in the way of good rest. But what do you have agency over regarding your rest? Could you find ways to do your homework earlier in the day? Can you be more conscious to give your cares and concerns to God when you crawl into bed so that you can rest? (And if someone chooses a bedtime for you, count yourself fortunate because it means you have permission to sleep!)

One way we have agency over our rest is by incorporating activities into our evening that make rest more accessible. Reading, spending time outdoors, praying, and actively calming our thoughts can all contribute to a better night's rest.

> Father, I don't have complete agency over my rest, but surely there are some things I can do to make it more possible. Please show me what changes I can make. Amen.

WORTH EVERY SECOND

You rise up early, and go to bed late, and work hard for your food, all for nothing. For the Lord gives to His loved ones even while they sleep.
PSALM 127:2

Related to agency over our rest is agency over our schedules.

You're probably familiar with the idea of decluttering—removing clutter from your home in order to free up space to create a calmer atmosphere. Did you know it's also a good idea to declutter your calendar?

Look at your schedule. What can or could you eliminate to create more space in your life? What activities or habits no longer serve your greatest priorities? Do you currently have commitments that are draining your time and energy without providing meaningful returns?

Obviously, you can't cut school, church, family time, or discipleship. But could you cut back on entertainment, nonessential obligations, or activities that no longer serve their original purpose? A good place to start when decluttering your calendar is by asking this question: *What are my greatest values and goals, and what in my life doesn't currently serve those purposes?*

The answer to that question may require an honest conversation with your parents. They may have good input on what can or can't be cut from your life to create more time for rest and growth.

> Father, please help me see where I'm investing my time unwisely or engaging in activities that don't contribute to my spiritual growth. Amen.

TRY, TRY AGAIN

Love does not do the wrong thing. Love never thinks of itself. Love does not get angry. Love does not remember the suffering that comes from being hurt by someone.
1 CORINTHIANS 13:5

We all make mistakes, so let's talk about them.

We discussed in an earlier devotion about how we respond to others. But what happens when *we* make a mistake? What happens when we say or do something unkind to someone? What happens when we allow anxiety to make our choices for us?

The answer is simple but not always easy: we repent, correct, and try again.

Repentance doesn't need to be fancy or impressive. Simply say something such as "I'm sorry for my actions/words recently. I realize that what I did/said was hurtful, and I ask you to forgive me." And if there's something you can do to make it right, do it.

Then, *move on*.

When we allow ourselves to wallow or get stuck in our past, we actually make the mistake even worse than it was originally. Mistakes do not define us. They are not labels we wear for eternity. We acknowledge them, apologize for them, learn from them, and then move on from them.

> Father, I do not want to allow my mistakes to define me or to hold me captive in shame and regret. Please help me respond correctly when I hurt someone, and then help me move past it. Amen.

WORD FOR WORD

Put out of your life these things also: anger, bad temper, bad feelings toward others, talk that hurts people, speaking against God, and dirty talk.
COLOSSIANS 3:8

Our words hold incredible power. In fact, Edward Bulwer-Lytton—an English author who lived two hundred years ago—famously said, "The pen is mightier than the sword." The Bible says similar things, including, "Death and life are in the power of the tongue" (Proverbs 18:21).

So, let's talk about critical words—both the words we say to and about others and the words we say to and about ourselves. Because both matter to God.

Whether or not we realize it, we are using critical words when we gossip about our friends, exclude certain classmates, express harsh or judgmental comments online, argue with our siblings, or fight with our parents. We're also using critical words when we criticize the body, mind, or talents God gave us.

Criticism, whether directed toward others or ourselves, actually leads to heightened stress and negative emotions. It often escalates conflict and hinders good communication.

God wants us to use words that uplift, encourage, and edify others.

As the well-known saying goes, "in a world where you can be anything, be kind."

> Father, You created every person on this planet and care deeply about each one. Help me honor and never harm people with my words. Amen.

IN ADDITION

The plan in a man's heart is like water in a deep well, but a man of understanding gets it out.
PROVERBS 20:5

Fighting anxiety and depression isn't all about *eliminating* things. It can also be about *adding* things.

Ephesians 4 contains what Bible teachers call the "put off and put on principle."

First, we put off anything in our lives that doesn't please God. This could include attitudes, habits, and behaviors that hinder our growth and closeness with God. We honestly examine our lives and ask God to help us identify issues such as pride, selfishness, fear, and bitterness. We confess anything to God that we need to acknowledge and intentionally let go of those things through confession, repentance, and surrender.

Second, we put on anything that pleases God. It isn't enough to eliminate what isn't helpful. We must add what is helpful. So we put on the virtues and qualities of Jesus—love, humility, kindness, and patience. We allow God and His Word to shape our attitudes, actions, and relationships.

There are three specific things we need to pursue: meaning, purpose, and community. In the following pages, let's look briefly at each.

> Father, as I learn to let go of old patterns and unhelpful mindsets, help me create room for new attitudes and behaviors that line up with Your truth. Amen.

REAL MEANING

O man, He has told you what is good. What does the Lord ask of you but to do what is fair and to love kindness, and to walk without pride with your God?
MICAH 6:8

We should pursue *meaning*.

Pursuing meaning isn't the same thing as doing something impressive. What is impressive to God is rarely the same thing as what is impressive to people.

To pursue meaning means we ask the question: *Why did God put me on this earth?*

Simple answer: God put you on this earth to glorify Him and enjoy Him forever.

My prayer for my daughter is the same as my prayer for you—that you would learn to do what is fair and to love kindness and to walk without pride with your God. If you spend your life in pursuit of these things, you will have a life of meaning no matter what else does or does not happen.

Pursuing meaning with our lives involves choosing joy in everyday experiences. It means being present and appreciating the simple things that others may miss in their attempts to find happiness in what they own or who they know.

You have everything you need to pursue a life of meaning.

Father, please help me to do what is fair, to love kindness, and to walk humbly with You. I know that my life would be full of meaning. Amen.

ON PURPOSE

But you are a chosen group of people. You are the King's religious leaders. You are a holy nation. You belong to God. He has done this for you so you can tell others how God has called you out of darkness into His great light.
1 PETER 2:9

We should pursue *purpose*.

Pursuing purpose can be a powerful weapon in our battle against anxiety.

When pursuing purpose, start by looking at what God has gifted you to do. Are you good with little kids? Do you enjoy music? Are you artistic? What skills or talents do you have that could be used to make a positive impact in the world?

Finding your purpose can happen by asking yourself this question: *Where do my skills and passions intersect with the world's great need?* Finding your purpose can take time, but it's a worthwhile effort. You may need to try different things and talk to trustworthy adults in your life.

When we discover what our purpose is, we can more easily reject the idea that we need to be good at everything and instead focus on what God has for our lives specifically.

> Father, as I look for purpose, please help me to remember that Your timing is perfect and Your plans for my life are greater than my own. Amen.

COMMUNITY CREATES STABILITY

We ask you, Christian brothers, speak to those who do not want to work. Comfort those who feel they cannot keep going on. Help the weak. Understand and be willing to wait for all men. Do not let anyone pay back for the bad he received. But look for ways to do good to each other and to all people.
1 THESSALONIANS 5:14–15

We should pursue *community*.

In community, we learn that other people struggle too, and we learn to encourage one another and bear one another's burdens. You can learn to help others, and others can learn to help you.

While you could join a club or an organization—such as sports, arts, music, debate, or volunteering—this decision could add more to your already full schedule. The most important community you can pursue is your local church.

You don't need to wait until you're older to pursue a good church community. God has already gifted you with talents and abilities that would make you an important contributor *right now*.

> Father, help me never take for granted the gift of the church. Instead, help me treasure and cherish her as a good gift from You. Amen.

BRAIN SCIENCE

For God did not give us a spirit of fear. He gave us a spirit of power and of love and of a good mind.
2 Timothy 1:7

Did you know that by changing your habits you can change your brain? This is good news!

Science says you can change the circuitry of your brain by what you practice. In other words, we have incredible power to reshape our minds through intentional actions and behaviors.

Teen brains—especially—are remarkably adaptable, capable of forming new connections and rewiring themselves based on experiences and habits.

So, if you don't like the thoughts and habits you currently have, you can work to change them!

In earlier devotions, we talked about the dangers of engaging in self-destructive habits and behaviors. One very practical reason to avoid these behaviors is because we can actually create well-worn neural pathways that deepen our anxiety.

On the other hand, replacing those harmful habits with good habits and practices can forge new pathways that promote growth.

One important note: Changing our habits and rewiring our brains take time, effort, and patience. It's not an overnight process, much as we would like it to be. But it can be done!

> Father, thank You for giving me the ability to grow and change with Your help. I want to honor You with my thoughts and habits. Amen.

HABITS THAT MAKE HOPE POSSIBLE

Do not let yourselves get tired of doing good. If we do not give up, we will get what is coming to us at the right time.
GALATIANS 6:9

There are habits that help make hope possible.

If you want to master a habit, the key is to start with repetition, not perfection. Striving to be perfect can often lead us to paralysis or discouragement. Perfection in any effort is an unrealistic standard that is generally impossible to meet. Wanting to be perfect often results in frustration and makes it easier for us to give up entirely.

Instead of aiming for perfection, we should learn to reach for repetition. Imagine that you want to start the regular habit of reading your Bible (a very good habit with great rewards!). Instead of setting as your goal, "I will read my Bible every single day and never miss," seek to read your Bible as many days in a row as possible. If you miss a day, start again. Seek to read your Bible for a longer stretch of days than you did before.

Aiming for repetition instead of perfection allows room for mistakes and gradual improvement.

In the following devotions, let's talk about some important and practical habits that could make hope possible in your life.

> Father, help me set down the impossibly high standard of perfectionism and instead work toward consistency through Your strength. Amen.

RE: THINKING

Christian brothers, keep your minds thinking about whatever is true, whatever is respected, whatever is right, whatever is pure, whatever can be loved, and whatever is well thought of. If there is anything good and worth giving thanks for, think about these things.
Philippians 4:8

One habit that makes hope possible: *guarding your thoughts.*

Our thoughts are not neutral. They hold incredible power and influence over our feelings, beliefs, and actions. Ongoing negative thoughts can contribute to fear and anxiety, while positive thoughts can cultivate confidence, resilience, and joy.

Our thoughts are like a train—they take us places, whether or not we realize we're traveling. If we consistently think unhelpful thoughts, the train will take us to places of heartache, fear, and anxiety. But if we take every thought captive and choose to think about what is true, right, and pure, then the train will take us to places of hope and resilience.

When we recognize the impact our thoughts have on our lives, we can choose to make changes, notice patterns, and replace unhelpful thoughts with constructive thoughts.

This isn't about the power of positive thinking or being happy, happy, happy all the time. We don't see either of those in the Bible. But this is about paying close attention to the thoughts that rule our lives and emotions.

> Father, please give me the courage to think carefully about my thoughts. Amen.

WHEN YOU NEED HELP

Two are better than one, because they have good pay for their work. For if one of them falls, the other can help him up. But it is hard for the one who falls when there is no one to lift him up.
ECCLESIASTES 4:9–10

Another habit that makes hope possible: *seeking help* when you need it.

Seeking help is not a sign of weakness but of courage. It is never a bad thing to seek help from the right people.

Asking for help from trusted mentors and friends gives us access to fresh perspectives, practical advice, and emotional support. Often what we're feeling and facing seems much bigger to us in the moment than it actually is.

When you need help: (1) identify a trusted person; (2) practice what you want to say; (3) find the right time and place for a private conversation; (4) be as clear and specific as you can about what you need; and (5) be open to what they suggest.

Be sure to give the person you talk to the time to process your request. If that person cannot help, don't give up. Go to another trusted person in your life.

Father, thank You that I do not need to face hard things by myself. When I need help, please give me the courage to ask for it. Amen.

WRITE IT DOWN

The works of the Lord are great. All who find joy in them try to understand them.
PSALM 111:2

Another habit that makes hope possible: *journaling.*

Journaling has been one of the greatest tools of transformation in my life. Journaling has equipped me to find joy in the works of God and to try to understand them. So I carry a notebook and record what I call "random thoughts" as I notice things or learn things throughout the day. I've journaled thousands of pages in the last few years alone.

Writing things down is a powerful process. Journaling provides a place to explore and process our thoughts, emotions, and experiences. When we identify what we believe by putting words on a page, what's in our hearts and minds becomes more visible to us.

Journaling enables us to watch for patterns. In an earlier devotion, I asked what triggers your anxiety or depression. If you don't know that answer, journaling is a good way to figure that out. What goes well? What doesn't go well? For example, if you're too busy to write anything down for a few days, maybe that is a signal *you're too busy*.

> Father, thank You for giving me tools to help me respond in ways that please You. Amen.

COMING CLEAN

The sorrow that God uses makes people sorry for their sin and leads them to turn from sin so they can be saved from the punishment of sin. We should be happy for that kind of sorrow, but the sorrow of this world brings death.
2 CORINTHIANS 7:10

Another habit that makes hope possible: *repenting*.

Repentance refers to an event in which we understand that our behavior has been wrong and feel compelled to ask for forgiveness and pursue change so that our relationship with God and others can be restored.

We should have as a goal in our lives to keep short accounts with God and others, which means we should be quick to address and resolve conflicts, offenses, or sins that happen in our relationships. It means we should practice regular forgiveness and open communication rather than allowing hurts and offenses to fester or accumulate.

Repentance is one of the hardest things God tells us to do, but it is also one of the most healing and transformative.

Important to note: Genuine repentance always involves more than just our words. It requires a sincere commitment to change and to take the appropriate actions necessary to fix any harm that has been caused.

Father, I know that repentance can go a long way toward making things right and can ultimately lead to growth and godliness. Help me have the humility to repent when necessary. Amen.

GUILTY AS CHARGED

It will not go well for the man who hides his sins, but he who tells his sins and turns from them will be given loving-pity.
PROVERBS 28:13

Speaking of repentance, what is *productive guilt*?

First, let's just acknowledge that even good guilt is uncomfortable. It can feel like uneasiness or heaviness in our chests or stomachs. We can experience tension or agitation when feeling guilty for something we've done.

But just because guilt *feels* bad doesn't always mean it *is* bad. Guilt can give us a strong desire to seek forgiveness or to fix a situation.

Productive guilt prompts reflection, remorse, and repentance. Good guilt ultimately helps us make changes to our behavior that lead to growth and godliness.

Productive guilt can motivate us to take responsibility, to apologize, to seek reconciliation, or to make things right. This type of guilt is really a gift in our lives from God, who wants us to be right with Him and with others.

Guilt is never the end goal. The end goal is repentance that leads to restoration and change. And guilt can be a useful tool to help us desire those good things.

Now that we've seen what productive guilt looks like, let's look at *unproductive guilt*.

> Father, thank You for guilt that helps me recognize when I've acted in a way that goes against what You've commanded. Help me respond correctly. Amen.

GUILT TRIP

No, Christian brothers, I do not have that life yet. But I do one thing. I forget everything that is behind me and look forward to that which is ahead of me.
PHILIPPIANS 3:13

What is *unproductive guilt*?

Unproductive guilt is a sense of guilt that serves no helpful purpose and actually hinders your growth. Where productive guilt can help us see where we need to repent and change, unproductive guilt often distorts reality.

Examples of unproductive guilt can be excessively thinking about or blaming ourselves for past mistakes or personal weaknesses, taking responsibility for events or outcomes outside our control, or feeling guilt for surviving a traumatic event or loss when others did not (also known as *survivor's guilt*).

Unproductive guilt lives in the past, dwelling on situations or conversations that could have gone differently. Unproductive guilt loves to consider "what if" scenarios—mercilessly rehashing what could have gone differently if something had been said or done differently.

Good guilt—as we saw in the preceding devotion—is healthy and helpful. It's a gift from God that prompts us to get right with people we've hurt and make better choices in the future. But unproductive guilt keeps us stuck.

> Father, please help me learn to see the difference between the type of guilt that You desire and the type of guilt that serves no helpful purpose. Amen.

NOT GUILTY

"If you forgive people their sins, your Father in heaven will forgive your sins also."
MATTHEW 6:14

Let's discuss how forgiveness is both a process and a promise.

First, as a reminder, you aren't ever expected to put yourself in danger or in any sort of harm's way. The commands in scripture to forgive are never meant to allow abuse to go unhandled. If you are being hurt by someone, tell a trusted adult.

But when it comes to the minor, hurtful frustrations caused by others. . .

- *Forgiveness is a process.* We acknowledge the harm caused by someone else's actions. We accept their apology. We let go of negative emotions or the desire to seek revenge. And we welcome the opportunity to rebuild trust (if the situation is safe).

- *Forgiveness is also a promise.* Forgiveness is our commitment that we won't hold on to resentment toward the person who wronged us. It's a choice to let go of grudges and rehashing of the wrongdoing. When we forgive, we're essentially promising to let it go and not bring it back up again.

Forgiveness is not a promise to *forget*. It is a commitment to release the burden of negative thoughts or feelings associated with the person we have forgiven.

> Father, as You have forgiven me, please help me learn to forgive those who sin against me. Amen.

COSTLY LOVE

You must be kind to each other. Think of the other person. Forgive other people just as God forgave you because of Christ's death on the cross.
EPHESIANS 4:32

What happens when someone wrongs us and chooses to repent?

We talked about forgiveness in the last devotion, but are we required to forgive? Here are a few thoughts:

First, we should always strive to imitate God's forgiveness in our relationships with other people. God has forgiven us, and so we should seek to forgive others.

Second, we should respond with humility. If someone extends a genuine apology, we should demonstrate a willingness to extend forgiveness, reflecting the same generous spirit God has shown to us when we repent to Him.

Third, we should communicate clearly. If you have things you need to say to clear the air, you should express your thoughts in a clear and honest way.

Fourth, we should set healthy boundaries. Forgiveness doesn't condone or enable harmful behavior. In every situation, it's important to consider the context and extent of the offense, seeking wisdom from trusted parents or mentors if necessary.

But we should always remember that God has forgiven us when we decide how to move forward with others.

> Father, forgiveness is some of the hardest work You've asked me to do. Please give me wisdom and strength to obey. Amen.

SORRY, NOT SORRY

*"Those who show loving-kindness are happy,
because they will have loving-kindness shown to them."*
MATTHEW 5:7

What happens when someone wrongs us and doesn't repent?

This situation can be really hard. The ache we feel in our hearts when someone fails to own the pain they've caused is a weight we all carry at some point in our lives. It's natural to long for the healing that can come with heartfelt repentance, but what do we do when the apology never arrives?

First, talk to God about it. He sees and knows everything and can help with the disappointment and hurt.

Second, consider the person who hasn't offered the apology. Maybe they aren't even aware of the depth of hurt they've caused. We remember that God loves that person too.

Third, let go of the need for the apology. Letting go doesn't remove the guilt or the offense, but it enables us to break free from the prison of unmet expectations. Letting go is not something we do for the other person as much as it's something we do for our own good.

While an apology from the offender would be ideal, it's important to remember that the lack of an apology doesn't diminish the hurt or invalidate the experience.

> Father, I know You can heal my heart and help me move forward with or without an apology from the person who hurt me. Help me trust You with this. Amen.

THIS ONE THING

*Come close to God and He will come close to you.
Wash your hands, you sinners. Clean up your
hearts, you who want to follow the sinful ways
of the world and God at the same time.*

JAMES 4:8

Another habit that makes hope possible: *spending time daily with God.*

One of the wisest things you can do is make time with God a central part of your daily life. Set aside dedicated time to engage with God in heartfelt conversation, expressing gratitude, seeking guidance, and praying for others.

Read the Bible for yourself, meditate on its truth, and seek to understand what God does and doesn't say. Don't take someone else's word for it. Read it. Reflect on it. Apply it.

Sometimes teens believe it will get easier to establish Bible reading and prayer habits when they're older, but I promise that's not true. The earlier you build these habits, the better.

If you're ready to take your Bible reading and prayer seriously, find an accountability partner—someone with whom you commit to check in regularly with updates on how you're doing.

In the fight against anxiety and depression, spending daily time with God is truly one of the best choices you can make for yourself. We'll discuss this daily habit next.

> Father, help me recognize the significance of these practices and carve out dedicated time every day to spend with You. Amen.

WORTH READING

Your words were found and I ate them. And Your words became a joy to me and the happiness of my heart. For I have been called by Your name, O Lord God of All.
JEREMIAH 15:16

One way we spend time with God daily: *reading the Bible.*

Can we just take a moment to talk about the incredible gift we have in God's Word? It's not a dusty old book but a living, breathing testament of love and wisdom inspired by a Creator who knows you personally.

The Bible has survived generations of men throughout history who have sought to destroy it—to silence its words and extinguish its power. But, against all human odds, the Bible has not only survived but thrived. It continues to change hearts and impact lives and can do the same for you.

So, when you read your Bible, don't just read it like you would a homework assignment—something to check off the list or say you've done it. Read the words like they were written just for you by someone who loves you very much.

As you read, take notes. Write down what you learn about God as you engage with the text. Ask God to show you what you need to discover. He will.

> Father, please help me never to allow distractions, busyness, or the cares of this world to stop me from reading the Bible faithfully. Amen.

IN MEMORY

*Your Word have I hid in my heart,
that I may not sin against You.*
PSALM 119:11

Another habit that makes hope possible: *memorizing verses*.

Memorizing verses from the Bible gives us a spiritual arsenal with which to fight anxiety and depression. When we have specific verses stored in our hearts and minds, we can more easily and quickly access them, thinking about them in moments of fear and uncertainty.

Even the process of memorizing helps us engage our minds and replace our anxious thoughts with biblical truth. We can't focus on multiple things at one time—it's humanly impossible. So either we focus on our fear and anxiety or we focus on Jesus. And memorizing Bible verses is one way we can focus on Jesus.

Then, after we've committed a verse to memory, God can bring that verse to our minds in a moment when we need to be reminded of its truth or comforted by its assurance.

Wondering what Bible verses you could memorize to help you fight anxiety? This book is filled with verses that would be good and helpful to memorize for moments of fear or anxiety.

Father, I recognize the importance of hiding Your Word in my heart. Please help me make memorization a priority so I can truly meditate on Your words day and night. Amen.

SELECTIVE HEARING

Let the teaching of Christ and His words keep on living in you. These make your lives rich and full of wisdom. Keep on teaching and helping each other. Sing the Songs of David and the church songs and the songs of heaven with hearts full of thanks to God.
COLOSSIANS 3:16

In a world filled with misinformation and constant noise, filling our minds with truth is essential to fighting anxiety.

We talked in an earlier devotion about guarding our thoughts. One practical way we do this is by listening to good music that points our hearts and minds to what God says is *true*.

It is hard—if not impossible—to worry and worship at the same time. It's hard to panic if we're praying. So even before you feel like doing it, turn on some helpful, truth-filled music. Praise God for who He is and what He has done.

When we listen to music that is filled with truth about how good God is, we redirect our focus away from anxious and unhelpful thoughts and are more easily able to reframe our perspective and place our trust in the one who sustains.

Good music filled with truth is a gift, and it's available to you when you need it.

> Father, thank You for the gift of good music. Help me intentionally listen to songs that point my heart to You. Amen.

REMEMBER THIS

*I will give thanks to the Lord with all my heart.
I will tell of all the great things You have done.*
PSALM 9:1

Another habit that makes hope possible: *remembering*.

On good days, we know God has been faithful to us. But on bad days, it's easy to experience spiritual amnesia. Amnesia is a condition characterized by either temporary or permanent memory loss. It can happen as a result of head injury or trauma.

Spiritually, we can have a sort of amnesia too. One day we can praise God for all of His goodness to us, and the next day we can wonder if we're alone and if God even cares.

One instruction given throughout the Bible is to remember what God has done for us in the past so that we don't lose hope when we face present troubles. When we remember what God has done for us in the past, we anchor our faith to His faithfulness. We see that God who has been faithful to us in the past will continue to be faithful in the future.

We can practice remembering by writing things down, by starting a gratitude journal, by creating traditions on important days, or by intentionally talking to our friends or family about God's faithfulness in our lives.

> Father, help me to remember what You have done. You have been good and faithful. Amen.

WALK BY FAITH

*God bought you with a great price. So honor
God with your body. You belong to Him.*
1 CORINTHIANS 6:20

Another habit that makes hope possible: *exercising*.

Exercise was given to us by God as a tool with numerous physical and psychological benefits. Often we think of exercise as something to help us get healthier or look stronger. But exercise is so much more than *how we look*.

Engaging in regular physical activity releases important mood-boosting chemicals in our bodies called *endorphins*, which help regulate cortisol, the stress hormone. These chemicals are very helpful for anxiety and depression. Exercise also contributes to better sleep, which is deeply beneficial for pursuing greater mental health. Exercise provides a healthy outlet for pent-up energy and creates mental clarity.

I have specific practices I do on low days. When I need to stop the unhelpful thoughts in my head, I often go for a walk. The goal on these walks isn't to burn calories or set records. The goal is to move the stress *through* and *out* of my body by moving.

Going on walks—especially on low days—is one of the best decisions we can make.

Father, help me to use the tools You have given me to fight unhelpful thoughts and feelings. I can't do everything, but I can do something. Amen.

COME AND SEE

The deep places of the earth are in His hand. And the tops of the mountains belong to Him. The sea is His, for He made it. And His hands made the dry land. Come, let us bow down in worship. Let us get down on our knees before the Lord Who made us.
PSALM 95:4–6

One of the ways we consistently fight anxiety is by learning to recognize what is *life-giving* and what is *life-depleting*. Here's a quick example of each.

First: *life-depleting*. Endless screens, notifications, and virtual interactions have a unique way of leaving us feeling mentally and emotionally empty. Constant exposure to social media and digital platforms can actually contribute to our feelings of anxiety or depression.

Second: *life-giving*. Nature is one of the most life-giving resources at our fingertips. Spending time outside has been linked to better brain function, improved concentration, and greater creativity. Being in nature helps us recover from ongoing mental fatigue.

My advice: find something you enjoy doing outside. Maybe it's reading a book, taking a walk, drawing, riding a bike. Look for an outdoor hobby until you find something you enjoy.

> Father, please give me a love and gratitude for the gift of being outdoors. Help me slow down and savor the sights, sounds, and scents of nature. Teach me to look for Your fingerprints in creation. Amen.

GO OUTSIDE

*When I look up and think about Your heavens,
the work of Your fingers, the moon and the stars,
which You have set in their place, what is man, that You
think of him, the son of man that You care for him?*
PSALM 8:3–4

Endless research says the same thing: technology drains; nature restores.

Yet, studies show that we're spending less time outdoors than any previous generation of human beings. Our busy lifestyles and endless stream of indoor entertainment can leave us little to no time to enjoy nature.

But two things in this life have the unique power to restore our weary souls: (1) time in God's Word and (2) time in God's creation.

Whether or not you enjoy being outdoors, unplugging from technology and stepping outside—to breathe in fresh air and immerse yourself in the gift of nature that God made—can relax your body and calm your racing mind. Nothing recharges like nature.

Go outside, be impressed by nature, and remind yourself that the God who made the big blue sky is the same God who takes a deep and unwavering interest in your life as well.

Bottom line: every day your soul needs to engage with creation.

> Father, thank You for the beauty and diversity of the outdoors. Help me appreciate it as a place where I can learn more about You and marvel at Your handiwork. Amen.

CAN YOU IMAGINE?

The Holy Writings say, "No eye has ever seen or no ear has ever heard or no mind has ever thought of the wonderful things God has made ready for those who love Him."
1 CORINTHIANS 2:9

Anxiety loves to imagine how many ways something could go wrong.

What if nobody wants to be my friend?
What if I don't get accepted into the college I want?
What if I lose somebody I love?

These are powerful thoughts, no question about it. So if it's in our power to imagine worst-case scenarios, it must also be in our power to imagine best-case scenarios.

What if God chooses to meet my need in a spectacular way?
What if God said no to my request because He's planning something far better?
What if His plans for my life are wonderful?

As said before, this isn't the power of positive thinking or setting unrealistic expectations. This is simply imagining better. This is believing that God is up to something good in your life—that the same God who accepted a little boy's sack lunch and used it to feed thousands can take what looks impossible in your life and do something extraordinary.

Father, please help me use the imagination You've given me to envision a future filled with hope. I know You will always be with me. Amen.

CHANGE IS HARD

*If you do not have wisdom, ask God for it.
He is always ready to give it to you.*
JAMES 1:5

Making changes typically feels wrong at first. We are wired to want to stay stubbornly in the same spot, yet change usually happens outside our comfort zones.

Doing what feels unfamiliar can cause us to question our decisions.

Maybe it would be easier just to do what I've always done.

Maybe it would be easier just to say yes instead of saying no when I should.

Maybe it would be easier to keep eating lunch with the same girls instead of meeting someone new.

Maybe I should keep my fears to myself instead of asking for help.

Most of us prefer what is familiar—even if what is familiar has been hurtful or unhealthy. But here's the good news about making changes. If we stick to what we know to be good and right, eventually those choices will become what is most familiar. Here are three things to remember:

- Hard choices aren't always bad choices.
- The comfort zone isn't always the right zone.
- Just because it feels wrong at first doesn't mean it is wrong.

> Father, please give me the courage to face the challenges that come with making good changes. Help me to overcome fear, resistance, and uncertainty. Amen.

LEARNING TO SURF

"God is not a man, that He should lie. He is not a son of man, that He should be sorry for what He has said. Has He said, and will He not do it? Has He spoken, and will He not keep His Word?"
NUMBERS 23:19

Life is seasonal.

You may remember from science class that tides, primarily influenced by the gravitational pull of the sun and moon, create a rhythmic rise and fall of the ocean's surface. As the moon orbits the earth, its gravitational force creates waves that get bigger or smaller depending on the schedule.

Life—like the waves of the ocean—is also seasonal. Hard times will come and hard times will go. Understanding how life works doesn't necessarily make the waves enjoyable, but it means we understand them for what they are, and we hold on for better days.

Learn to ride the waves. Learn to accept that change is a natural part of life, and then practice learning to adjust to new situations or circumstances.

Here are two things we can be confident of: the waves will come and go, and God will be faithful through them all.

Father, thank You for the gift of seasons. Help me appreciate that each season holds its own lessons, opportunities, and gifts. Teach me to trust You in every season. Amen.

BEFORE YOU QUIT

*I praise the Word of God. I have put my trust in God.
I will not be afraid. What can only a man do to me?*
PSALM 56:4

Speaking of learning to ride the waves, we know hard days will come. How do we respond?

- *Recognize the emotion.* Nowhere in the Bible are we commanded to deny that something is difficult or disappointing. If something hard or hurtful happened, acknowledge it.
- *Reflect on what happened.* Before you reach out to friends or family members to tell them what went wrong, talk to God about it. He wants to hear from you.
- *Reframe the difficulty.* Reframing is like putting on a new pair of glasses, enabling us to see our situation from a different perspective. On your next hard day, ask yourself, *What is God teaching me in this situation?*
- *Reach out for help.* If the events of your day were small enough that you can pray about them and move on, great! If you need help to process a situation or handle a hurt, don't hesitate to talk to a trusted person.

Hard days may feel all-consuming, but in reality, they are just a small part of your story. They are not the end. Keep trusting the one who holds you close.

> Father, I know hard days will come, but hard days are not permanent. Help me trust You for better days ahead. Amen.

TINY CHANGES

If the Holy Spirit is living in us, let us be led by Him in all things.
GALATIANS 5:25

Small choices add up to big change over time.

Small daily choices may seem like no big deal in the grand scheme of life—going for a walk, declining an invitation to a party, starting your morning by praying instead of checking social media, sitting with the new girl at lunch. But their cumulative impact over time can actually lead to remarkable, significant change. Our small choices end up shaping our habits, our relationships, and ultimately our lives—often in greater ways than the rarer big choice we make.

In other words, *small choices matter*.

Fighting anxiety and depression isn't magic. It requires repeating good choices, which turn into habits and then disciplines. And then, one day, we look back and realize we're living more peaceful lives for the glory of God.

Change doesn't happen overnight. Anything that matters takes time. But the accumulation of small, intentional choices made consistently can add up to a life less impacted by anxiety.

> Father, please help me make small choices and celebrate small victories, recognizing that they are paving the way for something bigger. Help me not to lose sight of what You can do with my choices if they are made to glorify You. Amen.

BACK TO THE FUTURE

I am sure that our suffering now cannot be compared to the shining-greatness that He is going to give us.
ROMANS 8:18

Whenever we're experiencing something difficult, it's hard to imagine that it will get better. This pain will not last forever, but how can we be sure?

I understand that things may feel tough right now. In the first devotion in this book, I told you that I believe you—because I do. I remember what it's like to be a teen girl—the peer pressure, the academic stress, the relationship management.

But hear me carefully: it will get better. You won't always feel overwhelmed. You won't always care what *those girls* think. Your emotions won't always feel like swirling storms. You won't always be a teen.

But even if you end up battling anxiety for years, if you are a follower of Christ, someday you will look at the face of Jesus and every hard thing you faced for the glory of God in this life will be worth it. Romans 8 tells us that the suffering we experience in this lifetime doesn't compare to how good things will be when we see Jesus.

Will it always be this way? No. Embrace the chaos, see it for what it is, and know that brighter days are coming.

Father, I know You will help me to heal what hurts. Help me believe with confidence that abundant life is available in the meantime. Amen.

THE REST OF THE STORY

The peace of God is much greater than the human mind can understand. This peace will keep your hearts and minds through Christ Jesus.
PHILIPPIANS 4:7

Continuing the idea that our anxiety will be healed someday: *perfect peace is coming, but present peace must be pursued.*

In other words, as followers of Jesus, we have the promise that complete and ultimate peace is coming when He returns and takes us home. And yet, in the meantime, we are still responsible to do our part in actively seeking and cultivating peace in our lives and circumstances.

Peace here on earth will never be perfect. There may always be a relationship or situation that could be improved, but we can learn to experience peace from God while we wait for His perfect peace to be ours for eternity.

While the Bible is not filled with formulas, Philippians 4:6 gives us a principle for pursuing the kind of peace we want in our lives: *"Do not worry. Learn to pray about everything. Give thanks to God as you ask Him for what you need."*

And the result? Peace greater than anything you can currently comprehend will keep your heart and mind through Christ Jesus.

> Father, thank You that this peace is completely available to me now. Help me pursue it as I give You my worries. Amen.

THANKS BE TO GOD

*Do not worry. Learn to pray about everything.
Give thanks to God as you ask Him for what you need.*
PHILIPPIANS 4:6

Gratitude is important in the fight against anxiety and depression.

One of the most famous verses in the Bible about anxiety, Philippians 4:6, links "Do not worry" with "Give thanks." And what the Bible links together, we should learn to link together too. These aren't just two random commands God threw into a verse like we might throw random items into a junk drawer. There is a holy link between *not worrying* and *giving thanks*.

One reason gratitude is powerful is because it helps us shift our focus away from what is lacking in our lives to what God has graciously and generously given to us already. We live in a world that often emphasizes scarcity and comparison, and gratitude is our active fight against either of those unhelpful mentalities.

Cultivating gratitude can happen in many different forms. It can include journaling, expressing thankfulness to others, or simply stopping to acknowledge things throughout our day that we are grateful for. But no matter how we cultivate gratitude, we should remember to thank God for everything since James 1:17 tells us that God is the giver of all good gifts.

> Father, I know You are the giver of everything good in my life. Thank You. Amen.

AN HONEST OFFERING

He gives us comfort in all our troubles. Then we can comfort other people who have the same troubles. We give the same kind of comfort God gives us.
2 CORINTHIANS 1:4

With so many teen girls battling anxiety, you have an opportunity to lead by example. What do you understand about anxiety and depression that you can now share with someone else who may be hurting?

Here's the thing: you have the unique opportunity to show others what it means to walk through anxiety with grace, strength, and resilience.

Leading by example means showing others it's okay to talk about anxiety. You can encourage your friends to share their stories, struggles, and victories. You can remind them that they aren't alone.

Leading by example doesn't mean you have to have all the answers or pretend to be perfect. You can demonstrate what it looks like to acknowledge your own limitations and still seek help when you need it.

You are fearfully and wonderfully made. Your story gives you the opportunity to share it with others and show your friends that there is hope and healing beyond anxiety's grip.

In the following devotions, let's look at four promises you can grab hold of as you move forward on this journey.

> Father, please show me girls in my life who
> I can encourage with the encouragement
> You have given me. Amen.

BETTER TOGETHER

Yes, even if I walk through the valley of the shadow of death, I will not be afraid of anything, because You are with me. You have a walking stick with which to guide and one with which to help. These comfort me.
PSALM 23:4

God will always be with you.

In every season, through every challenge, and in every joy—God will be present. God's presence in your life is steadfast and unwavering.

When life feels overwhelming and the weight of the world seems too much to bear, you are not alone. God is there. He sees your struggles, your fears, and your doubts. He is committed to walking with you through every season of your life.

When you make wrong choices or carry deep regrets, you can always turn to God. He will forgive and help you.

Even if the worst possible things you can imagine happen in your life, God will be with you.

So, my dear one, hold fast to the truth that God will be with you. Welcome the peace that comes from knowing you are never alone. Walk forward in confidence, knowing that the God who created the universe is by your side, every single step of the way.

> Father, thank You for Your promise that You will be with me no matter what. Amen.

FOLLOW THE LEADER

"Be strong and have strength of heart. Do not be afraid or shake with fear because of them. For the Lord your God is the One Who goes with you. He will be faithful to you. He will not leave you alone."
DEUTERONOMY 31:6

God will go ahead of you.

When you try something new, when you face a daunting challenge, when you take the twists and turns of life, God is already there. He prepares your path and guides your steps. *Every single one of them.* You never need to wonder if He knows or cares—He's already there.

Your heavenly Father is not a passive bystander in your life. He's an active participant in every detail—working behind the scenes for your good and for His glory. His love for you is so vast—so immeasurable—that He goes before you to make a way where there seems to be no way.

The classroom.
The doctor's office.
The youth group.
The conversation.
The move.
The job.

He's already there. And not just in the big or scary things. He is in every ordinary, seemingly insignificant part of your life as well.

Father, thank You for the certainty that nothing takes You by surprise. You are already ahead of me and aware of what's going to happen. Amen.

THE GOD WHO STAYS

He is working in you. God is helping you obey Him. God is doing what He wants done in you.
Philippians 2:13

God will never leave you or forsake you.

This truth is woven throughout the pages of scripture. In Deuteronomy 31:6 (ESV), Moses reminded the Israelites, "Be strong and courageous. Do not fear or be in dread of them, for it is the Lord your God who goes with you. He will not leave you or forsake you."

These words echo throughout the Bible, serving as a constant reminder of God's unwavering presence. This promise is not mere words on a page. It is an unwavering commitment from the heart of a faithful God.

God will never leave or forsake you. Others may leave; God will always stay.

God will *never* leave or forsake you. Not in good times or in bad.

God will never leave or forsake *you*. His promise is personal and permanent.

So take heart. In the moments when you can't see a way forward, remember that God is right there with you, holding you, carrying you if need be.

He is faithful, and His love for you knows no limits.

> Father, Your faithfulness is a rock on which I can build my life—a foundation that gives me security and hope. Thank You. Amen.

STRENGTH FOR TODAY

I pray that God's great power will make you strong, and that you will have joy as you wait and do not give up. I pray that you will be giving thanks to the Father. He has made it so you could share the good things given to those who belong to Christ who are in the light.
COLOSSIANS 1:11–12

God will make you strong and courageous.

Imagine that you are standing at the edge of a vast wilderness, facing challenges and uncertainties that seem impossible. Maybe it's a big dream you're longing to pursue. Maybe it's a difficult season that requires resilience and perseverance. Maybe it's a big step you're finally ready to take in your spiritual life.

But that small inner voice whispers, *You can't do it. You don't have what it takes.*

That is not the voice of God. God is the source of your strength and courage. He is the one who equips you with the tools you need to do His will. His power is made perfect in your weakness as you rely on Him.

You don't have to be your own strength and courage—God will give you exactly what you need.

Father, thank You for Your strength that carries me through the storms of life and upholds me in my moments of weakness so I can face whatever challenges come my way. Amen.

MY PRAYER FOR YOU

I pray that because of the riches of His shining-greatness, He will make you strong with power in your hearts through the Holy Spirit.
EPHESIANS 3:16

You made it. We've talked about a lot of things in this book, and here we are at the final devotion.

This is my prayer for you: That God would pour out the immeasurable riches of His glory on your life. That in the midst of life's deepest challenges and uncertainties, you would be anchored to the assurance of God's persistent love for you.

I pray that God would strengthen your innermost being, so that you would discover peace that surpasses even your own understanding, enabling you to navigate every decision in your life with clarity and grace.

Most of all, my prayer is that you would be rooted and grounded in God's love, drawing from it the unshakable confidence you need to do what God has asked you to do.

My prayer is that your life would be a testimony of God's immeasurable love and goodness, that your words and actions would reflect His character, drawing others to want to know the Jesus you love. I pray that your life—the way you handle every anxious moment—would be a beacon of light in a world that so desperately needs God.

So love God. Love God's Word. Love His people.
And you will be okay.

> Father, thank You for being a good and faithful God. I love You. Amen.

SCRIPTURE INDEX

OLD TESTAMENT

NUMBERS
23:19 .... p. 175

DEUTERONOMY
31:6 .... p. 183

JOSHUA
1:9 .... p. 30

1 CHRONICLES
29:11 .... p. 96

JOB
11:7–9 .... p. 89
23:8–9 .... p. 72

PSALMS
1:2 .... p. 51
4:8 .... p. 146
8:3–4 .... p. 172
9:1 .... p. 169
9:10 .... p. 83
13:5–6 .... p. 123
15:2–3 .... p. 141
18:30 .... p. 46
23:4 .... p. 182
25:4–5 .... p. 105
25:16 .... p. 117
27:3 .... p. 136
27:13–14 .... p. 112
31:24 .... p. 114
33:18 .... p. 21
34:8 .... p. 31
34:18 .... p. 134
37:5 .... p. 108

42:11 .... p. 111
46:1–2 .... p. 90
51:6 .... p. 58
51:12 .... p. 74
56:3 .... p. 26
56:4 .... p. 176
62:1–2 .... p. 143
62:8 .... p. 25
73:26 .... p. 135
90:12 .... p. 97
94:19 .... p. 133
95:4–6 .... p. 171
101:2 .... p. 61
101:3 .... p. 34
103:12–14 .... p. 131
111:2 .... p. 158
112:7 .... p. 127
119:11 .... p. 167
119:105 .... p. 50
121:3 .... p. 82
121:7–8 .... p. 23
127:2 .... p. 147
139:4 .... p. 64
139:12 .... p. 11
139:14 .... p. 33
139:23–24 .... p. 16
143:8 .... p. 106
145:18 .... p. 118
147:3 .... p. 91

PROVERBS
1:33 .... p. 15
3:5 .... p. 101

4:25–26	p. 142
9:9	p. 137
12:17	p. 60
15:22	p. 55
15:31	p. 128
17:22	p. 144
18:24	p. 56
19:21	p. 24
20:5	p. 150
25:27	p. 79
27:6	p. 19
27:10	p. 121
28:13	p. 160

ECCLESIASTES
4:9–10	p. 157

ISAIAH
26:3	p. 66
41:10	p. 12
53:5	p. 20
54:10	p. 44
55:8–9	p. 93

JEREMIAH
15:16	p. 166
17:7	p. 145

LAMENTATIONS
3:21–23	p. 113
3:24	p. 110

MICAH
6:8	p. 151

NAHUM
1:7	p. 22

ZEPHANIAH
3:17	p. 75

MALACHI
3:6	p. 92

NEW TESTAMENT

MATTHEW
5:7	p. 164
6:14	p. 162
6:26	p. 47
6:27	p. 9
6:34	p. 10
11:28	p. 98
11:28–30	p. 81

LUKE
6:27–28	p. 37
6:31	p. 80
8:17	p. 59

JOHN
8:32	p. 27
8:44	p. 71
14:27	p. 32
15:18	p. 129
16:33	p. 7, 17

ACTS
17:24–25	p. 102

ROMANS
5:5	p. 109
7:25	p. 45

8:18	p. 178
8:28	p. 67
8:37	p. 85
8:38–39	p. 70
12:12	p. 52
15:13	p. 84

1 Corinthians

2:9	p. 173
3:23	p. 63
6:19	p. 13
6:20	p. 170
7:17	p. 36
10:13	p. 29
10:24	p. 104
10:31	p. 40
13:5	p. 148
15:57	p. 139
16:14	p. 41

2 Corinthians

1:4	p. 181
4:17	p. 76
4:18	p. 28
5:7	p. 130
7:10	p. 159
10:5	p. 107
12:9	p. 119
12:10	p. 69

Galatians

1:10	p. 103
5:13	p. 138
5:14–15	p. 94
5:25	p. 177
6:2	p. 54
6:4–5	p. 39
6:9	p. 155

Ephesians

1:14	p. 87
1:19	p. 18
2:10	p. 48
3:16	p. 186
3:20–21	p. 99
4:23	p. 49
4:26	p. 78
4:32	p. 163
5:16–17	p. 124

Philippians

2:3	p. 14
2:13	p. 184
3:8	p. 35
3:13	p. 161
4:6	p. 180
4:7	p. 179
4:8	p. 156
4:19	p. 100

Colossians

1:11–12	p. 185
1:17	p. 95
3:8	p. 149
3:13	p. 120
3:15	p. 73
3:16	p. 168
3:23	p. 38
3:24	p. 43

1 Thessalonians

5:14–15	p. 153

5:17 .... p. 53

2 Timothy
1:7 .... p. 154
2:23 .... p. 125

Titus
2:8 .... p. 126

Hebrews
4:16 .... p. 132
10:23 .... p. 115
10:25 .... p. 122

James
1:5 .... p. 174
1:6 .... p. 65
1:17 .... p. 68
3:2 .... p. 42
4:8 .... p. 165
4:17 .... p. 140

1 Peter
1:3 .... p. 116
2:9 .... p. 152
5:7 .... p. 8

2 Peter
1:3 .... p. 88

1 John
1:8–9 .... p. 57
3:1 .... p. 86
3:18 .... p. 62
3:20 .... p. 77

MORE ENCOURAGEMENT FOR YOUR BEAUTIFUL SPIRIT!

You Belong
Devotions and Prayers for a Teen Girl's Heart

You Were Created with Purpose by a Loving, Heavenly Creator. . .You Belong!

This delightful devotional is a lovely reminder that you were created with purpose by a heavenly Creator. . .and that you belong—right here and now—in this world. 180 encouraging readings and inspiring prayers, rooted in biblical truth, will reassure your uncertain heart, helping you to understand that you're never alone and always loved. In each devotional reading, you will encounter the bountiful blessings and grace of your Creator, while coming to trust His purposeful plan for you in this world.

Flexible Casebound / 978-1-63609-169-3

Find This and More from Barbour Publishing at Your Favorite Bookstore or www.barbourbooks.com

BARBOUR
PUBLISHING